*D*espite their fishlike form and total commitment to living in the sea, whales and dolphins are mammals. They breathe air, bear their young live, and have hair. To scientists they are members of the order Cetacea. To the public, they can be as different as the graceful Atlantic spotted dolphin (left), or the friendly but warty humpback whale (above).

Whales are the stuff of legends. They are huge, powerful, and mysterious. Some we see often, yet we know little about them. Others prowl the vastness of the sea, unseen except by a fortunate few.

Herman Melville, in his famous novel "Moby Dick," said of the common dolphin, "...he always swims in hilarious shoals, which upon the broad sea keep tossing themselves to heavens like caps in a Fourth-of-July crowd." He added, "If you yourself can withstand three cheers at beholding these vivacious fish, then heaven help ye; the spirit of godly gamesomeness is not in ye." Today these lovely creatures, especially young ones, evoke the same feelings of delight.

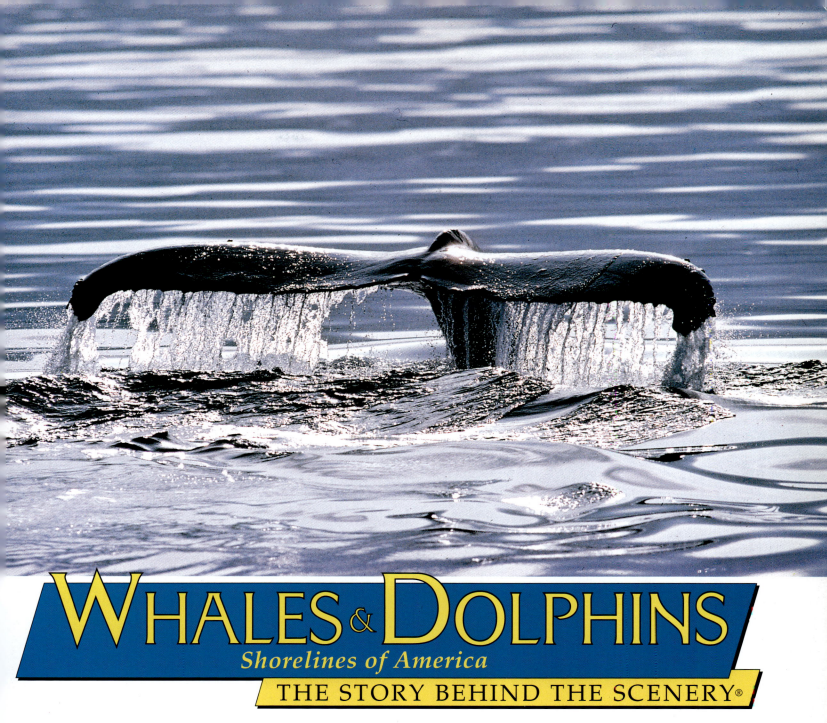

Whales & Dolphins
Shorelines of America
THE STORY BEHIND THE SCENERY®

by Peter C. Howorth

Peter C. Howorth, who also wrote *Channel Islands: The Story Behind the Scenery* and *Sharks: The Story Behind the Scenery*, is well known for his magazine articles about the sea. His volunteer work in rescuing marine mammals has been featured in many television productions, including a two-hour Cousteau special. Peter directs a nonprofit clinic for sick, injured, and orphaned marine mammals. Peter's clinic also rescues marine mammals caught in fishing nets or stranded on the beach. He participates in various research projects involving marine mammals as well.

Front cover: Breaching humpback, photo by F. Stuart Westmorland. Inside front cover: Atlantic spotted dolphin, photo by James D. Watt. Page 1: Warty humpback, photo by Peter C. Howorth. Pages 2/3: Gray whale feeding in kelp, photo by Howard Hall. Page 4: Common dolphins, photo by Peter C. Howorth. Page 5: Humpback tail, photo by Peter C. Howorth.

Book design by K. C. DenDooven. Edited by Mary L. Van Camp.

Fourth Printing • Revised Edition, 1994
WHALES & DOLPHINS, SHORELINES OF AMERICA: THE STORY BEHIND THE SCENERY.
© 1994 KC PUBLICATIONS, INC.
LC 94-75106. ISBN 0-88714-083-1.

WHALE. The word conjures up images of immense size and power, of gentleness or savagery, and of familiarity somehow shrouded in mystery, for this largest of creatures remains a stranger to us in many ways. Our understanding of the whale is nearly as fragmentary and elusive as the mist of its blow.

We know a little more about the dolphin, if only because its comparatively small size and gentle demeanor make it easier to handle. But both animals live in the trackless immensity of the sea, where human observers can only seize fleeting glimpses into their life.

Unfortunately, our legacy is to know more of their death than of their life; for we have hunted many of these creatures to near extinction. The killing continues even today. Dolphins and porpoises die in droves only because they follow tuna and salmon schools. Great whales still fall to the explosive harpoons of nations more interested in exploitation than conservation.

Some 40 tons of whale clear the surface as this humpback breaches off the Hawaiian coast. Humpbacks are perhaps the most acrobatic of whales, leaping out of the sea with only two or three flips of their mighty flukes. Off the California coast, one humpback breached more than 200 times over a two-hour period, perhaps setting a new record.

This short-finned pilot whale is closely related to the long-finned pilot whale. In the Atlantic, where their ranges overlap, the two species can be confused, but in the north Pacific, the short-finned pilot whale seems to be the only representative of its kind.

What we have discovered of *cetaceans* (whales, dolphins, and porpoises) is fascinating enough to open entirely new fields of inquiry. The study of whales is the ultimate challenge because nowhere on land are animals so huge and their environment so boundless.

Cetaceans have broken their ties with the land so effectively that their past is largely unknown to us. Even though they are mammals, they are so far removed from us on the evolutionary scale that merely describing them requires a different vocabulary. Common terrestrial terms often cannot do them justice.

The sea is their stronghold, because even a creature as large as a whale is hard to find there, especially if it wanders far from land in small groups. Even today, scientists feel that species unknown to us may roam the vast reaches of the sea. As recently as 1991, an entirely new species of whale was discovered in remote regions of the South Pacific.

The Largest Creatures on Earth

Before the mighty dinosaurs perished some 70 million years ago, a seemingly insignificant, insect-eating mammal had appeared. Soon, lacking competition from the giant reptiles, it prospered, using its peculiar attributes to singular advantage. Its warm blood and fur kept out the chill of the advancing ice ages.

This creature bore its young live and cared for them as they grew, ensuring the continuance of its kind. This mammal's relatively complex brain endowed it with acute senses and a blossoming intelligence unknown to its predecessors.

In time, this animal branched into two groups: the herbivores—plant-eaters, and the carnivores—flesh-eaters. These groups divided into many others, each to fill a particular ecological niche. Some, through selective adaptations, gradually returned to the sea. Such animals were probably evolutionary descendants of early *ungulates*, even-toed animals related to the cattle, sheep, and pigs of today.

The earliest known relatives of *cetaceans* appeared more than 50 million years ago. These *archaeocetes* ("ancient whales"), known as *Prozeuglodons*, were about the size of today's dolphins. They had well-developed teeth, probably for grasping small fish. Their nostrils, unlike those of terrestrial mammals, had gradually moved up along their head until they were midway between their snout and their cranium; thus they could breathe without lifting their head. Also, they could keep their eyes submerged for an uninterrupted view of their liquid environment.

Zeuglodons appeared some 10 million years later—slender, 70-foot-long creatures so reptilian in appearance that scientists first thought they were marine dinosaurs and dubbed them *Basilosaurus*, a name largely discounted today. Like their predecessors, the Zeuglodons were probably fish-eaters, for they had rows of dolphinlike teeth and blowholes on top of their head.

Such creatures flourished in the western portion of the ancient Tethys Sea, which overlapped the present Mediterranean. Later, this sea likely opened up to the Indian Ocean near the present Suez Canal, to the Baltic via Europe, and to the Central Atlantic between Europe and Africa. Another channel may have cut across Nigeria to the South Atlantic.

The fin whale, up to 80 feet long, is second only to the blue whale in size. Unlike all other mammals, its coloring is consistently different from one side to the next. The right side of its lower jaw is white, while the left is gray, like the rest of its body. Some researchers believe that such markings aid the whale in rounding up prey. They theorize that the whale can spook fish into a tight ball by circling a school with their white jaw showing, then reverse course, taking the fish unawares from their dark side.

The humpback whale is a relatively new species, at least in terms of geologic time. Among the largest of predators, it has no teeth. It feeds on shrimplike creatures and small fish, straining them out of its huge maw with its brushlike baleen plates. The humpback, like other baleen whales, probably evolved from ancient toothed whales, developing the baleen plates as a more efficient means of capturing large quantities of small prey items. Pleats along its throat expand, allowing the whale to gulp prodigious volumes of water.

Thus, the expanding sea allowed these primitive relatives of cetaceans to spread. Cetaceans would soon populate all the seas.

THE FIRST TRUE WHALES

What happened next is buried in the Early Oligocene rocks of 35 million years ago, for Zeuglodon seems to have reached an evolutionary dead end, or else any direct link it may have had to modern cetaceans is missing.

The next creatures to appear were very similar to some of today's. Called *Squalodonts* because their teeth resembled those of sharks ("squalus" means shark), they probably were the ancestors of at least one family of contemporary dolphins.

More than 26 million years ago, early relatives of modern baleen whales appeared. No older fossils have been unearthed to link these whales to their ancestors, but scientists believe they descended from ancient toothed whales. The ancestors of today's toothed whales did not appear until shortly after the early baleen whales, and their links to earlier forms are also buried in the past.

Of today's whales, the gray is probably most closely related to the ancient baleen whales. Fossil remains of grays perhaps as much as 200,000 years old have been found near San Pedro, California. Gray whales lived in the North Atlantic until several hundred years ago, then disappeared.

With so many missing fossil links, it seems surprising that even this comprehensive a cetacean history is known. Clues can be gleaned from other sources, however. For one thing, we know from embryological studies that developing cetaceans grow the hind limbs of terrestrial mammals, only to have them disappear as the fetus progresses. Even after they are born, cetaceans possess rudimentary pelvic bones. These are not without function, for even though they are buried in muscle tissue and are not connected to other bones, they do serve as an anchor for the male's reproductive organ.

Moreover, all cetaceans have teeth or tooth buds in the early stages of development. These disappear in the *mysticetes* ("moustache whales") to be replaced in function by baleen plates, brushlike structures for straining food from the water. Even cetacean blood provides clues to the past, for the composition of its serum protein resembles that of the ruminants, or cud-chewing animals. Also, cetacean stomachs are divided into three chambers.

Strangely enough, many cetaceans even behave like ruminants. They form groups called pods rather than herds. Some will even follow a leader to certain death. They can be curious or suspicious about anything new in their realm. Some use their head to butt other creatures. Males may even butt one another. Their mating is very brief, and the calves are able to move on their own shortly after they are born. Whether these traits are inherited or have developed out of necessity is unknown, but most of them do help these animals survive in a hostile environment.

As unfriendly as the sea may seem at times, it is the only place where animals as large as the great whales can survive. No bones are strong enough to support their weight on land; no limbs are powerful enough to move them. Indeed, no muscles are even tough enough to simply expand their chest for breathing—which is why whales die when they become stranded on beaches.

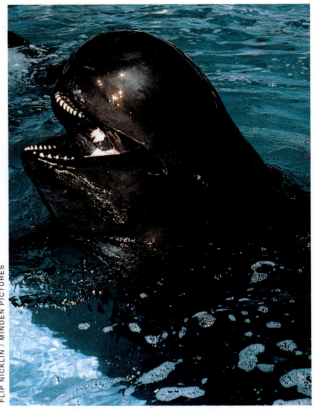

Pilot whales are apparently named for following leaders. This captive specimen only has to follow its trainer's lead.

Elephants seem large, but a whale's tongue can weigh more. The dinosaurs were huge; yet the biggest ones actually lived semiaquatic lives, their massive bulk supported in part by water. Only the sea could have spawned the great whales—only the sea can support them.

A Fishlike Mammal Emerges

Although Aristotle in his great wisdom recognized cetaceans as mammals, many subsequent observers did not. This was more a tribute to the extent that cetaceans had adapted to their environment than a lack of acumen on the observers' part, because they had scant opportunities for seeing the animals alive—as warm-blooded, air-breathing creatures.

Cetaceans are fishlike, although their tail flukes, or lobes, are horizontal rather than vertical. Halibut and other flatfish have similar tails, which are perfectly suited for rocketing upward from the sea floor to seize prey. In the case of cetaceans, the flukes allow the animals to swim to the surface to breathe, then return to the depths to feed. It seems strange that the flukes have no bones, but this is only a reflection of how well the cetaceans have adapted to their environment over the ages.

Whale calves stay close to their mothers for protection, nursing, and learning to survive in the hostile sea. At birth, a humpback calf is 12 to 14 feet long. When it is weaned in less than a year, it is twice that length and many times the weight. An adult humpback can weigh over 40 tons. Humpbacks usually give birth every two or three years. The gestation period is about 12 months. Sexual maturity is reached at about 7 years, and the humpback can live more than 50 years.

A gray whale calf slides onto its mother's back. Calves do this to snatch a moment of rest, and occasionally in an attempt to stay out of the reach of killer whales. Note the baleen showing in the youngster's mouth.

The common dolphin is a toothed cetacean. Its form is adapted for swiftness and agility. It has many vertebrae, allowing tremendous flexibility throughout most of its length. Its neck bones, however, are fused together so that its neck will remain rigid. This helps streamline its movements. Its fore limbs are modified into flippers, and the hind limbs have disappeared. The dolphin's brain is quite large. Much of it is geared toward interpreting sounds.

The flukes are driven by powerful muscles connected to the spine. Chevron-shaped bones on the underside of the last several vertebrae and spines on top provide additional surface area for the attachment of muscles. The spine itself has more vertebrae than the spine of most land mammals. Each vertebra is relatively short, and therefore allows tremendous flexibility. The neck vertebrae are sometimes fused together, however, so that head movements will not break the streamlined form of the animal.

The skull is massive, sometimes dominating one-third the length of the skeleton. Huge jaws account for most of the skull's length. The rib cage varies in cetaceans—whales generally have a comparatively small chest, while dolphins have a relatively large one. The rear ribs float—that is, they are not connected by a sternum. This allows for a tremendous expansion of their lungs as well as for the collapse of their lungs during deep dives.

The flippers, like our arms, are attached to the shoulder blade with a ball joint, but there the similarity ends, for the bones of the flipper form a rigid fin. The flippers are similar in function to the control surfaces on an airplane wing. They can be angled for diving or surfacing, or tilted independently for rolling or turning. Maximum speed is attained when they are flat against the body. When the flippers are fully extended, the animal slows down.

Some cetaceans have dorsal fins. Though not supported by bone, they are generally rather rigid and provide directional stability. Dorsals probably also make fast turns possible, acting much like a surfboard fin in preventing slippage.

The area forward of the tail also aids in turning, because it is usually flat and tall. This shape creates very little resistance, but provides quite a "bite" for turning. Like the dorsal fin, this ridge probably aids in directional stability, working like the keel of a boat. Its form also provides support for up-and-down tail movements and flexibility for turning.

The overall body shape of the cetacean is somewhere between a cigar and a teardrop. Designers of submarines have imitated this superior form to advantage.

The gray whale, like most baleen whales, has a smaller brain in relation to its body size than does the dolphin. Unlike toothed whales, baleen whales probably do not use sonar to locate prey, thus the part of their brain that would be used in interpreting sound waves is not well developed. Also, baleen whales have a comparatively small chest.

ILLUSTRATIONS BY JANN POPSON

The orca, or killer whale, is the most formidable predator on earth—next to humans. Capable of hunting down even a blue whale, the orca hunts in packs, with highly developed strategies. Some orca groups, or pods as they are called, feed almost entirely on fish. Others, especially transient groups, prey on marine mammals. Orcas range from the tropics to the poles. They can turn over ice cakes to tip seals into their grasp, or hunt down large sharks. Fortunately, they are rarely aggressive toward humans.

Monarchs of the Sea

It has been said that some cetaceans use their muscles several times more efficiently than any other mammal. One scientist even concluded that dolphins theoretically could not have enough muscle power to swim as fast as they do. He based his conclusions on the power required to move a rigid shape, patterned after a dolphin, through the water.

But no cetacean is rigid—therein lies the pitfall of his intriguing theory. Flexibility actually increases speed. The dolphin's thin porous outer layer of skin absorbs minute vibrations caused by turbulence created by water resistance. Moreover, the blubber layer, which streamlines the body shape, ripples as the animal accelerates, causing wrinkles to remain in certain places under high speed. The ridges correspond to low-pressure areas; the dimples to high-pressure regions. Thus, swirls of turbulence cannot form around the dolphin's body and reduce its speed.

As efficient as they are, dolphins are not as fast as many think. They can cut in toward the side of a fast-moving boat, then ride its bow wave, thus giving the illusion that they can easily travel at more than 20 knots (nearly 23 miles an hour). Most dolphins actually reach only 14 to 16 knots. The Dall porpoise exceeds 20 knots, but only in short sprints.

Bow-riding is a remarkable phenomenon in itself. Judging its speed with precision, the dolphin can burst in on the beam of a fast vessel and take up station just under the bow. The dolphin will position its flukes so the water upwelling from the bow will push against them, thus driving the animal forward with scant effort on its part. The dolphin thus planes along ahead of the bow wave, comfortably supported by the rush of water under its pectoral fins.

Some whales swim even faster than dolphins. The sperm whale probably reaches 20 knots, while the killer whale likely exceeds that. The huge blue may reach 30, and the sei (pronounced "say") may be faster yet.

ROBERT L. PITMAN / EARTHVIEWS

A study in speed, the slender northern right whale leaps just ahead of a research vessel. Often shy of boats, cetaceans sometimes will ride a bow wave.

Like a submarine bursting to the surface, this blue whale's head emerges in a huge splash. The head alone is some 30 feet long. Each blowhole is large enough to stick a leg into. When a blue whale decides to move fast, it can probably make 30 knots, a speed most ships would have trouble matching. The blue whale can also sustain an impressive speed for hours on end, unlike many smaller cetaceans. This blue whale was chasing another blue whale, perhaps in a dispute over territory, or in the heat of a mating effort.

A pod of sperm whales breaks the surface. Unique among cetaceans, these whales have odd, single blowholes on the left side of their heads. When they blow, the spray travels forward and to the left, making them easy to distinguish. Moby Dick, the fictional whale of Herman Melville fame, was a sperm whale.

While the speed of some cetaceans is impressive, their diving ability is even more so. A sperm whale can descend to at least three quarters of a mile and hold its breath for an hour. The killer whale can reach a depth of 3,400 feet, while the pilot whale can dive to 2,000 feet. Even the bottlenose dolphin can swim downward at least 1,000 feet.

How Can They Do It?

When a whale prepares to dive it inhales. Because its nostrils are on top of its head, it wastes no effort lifting its head to breathe, nor does it break its easy swimming rhythm. Its lungs are high on its body, which may ease the muscular effort required to expand them against the water pressure. The more relaxed the animal is, the more energy it can conserve for the dive. The exchange of gases in the lungs is nearly complete with each breath, whereas in humans, only 10 to 15 percent of the air is renewed with each breath.

When the whale dives, its blowhole clamps shut, sealing out water. Its epiglottis, near the base of its tongue, fits into the nasal passage, sealing it off so the animal can feed underwater even as it holds its breath.

Whale blood is rich in hemoglobin, which holds oxygen and carries it to the muscles and organs. The muscles are laced with myoglobin, which retains oxygen in the tissues. As the whale submerges, its heart rate slows, reducing the flow of blood to all but the vital organs and even storing some in an elaborate network of vessels called the *retia mirabilia* ("wonderful net"). This blood can then seep to the vital organs as the minutes pass underwater.

Meanwhile, the muscles may function without oxygen from the blood, obtaining it instead from the myoglobin in the tissues. Carbohydrates can be oxidized to release energy, with lactic acid as a byproduct. The animal is highly tolerant of lactic acid, the compound that produces muscle fatigue. When the whale takes in oxygen again on the surface, the lactic acid is broken down. Carbon dioxide from the whale's metabolic processes is also eliminated at this time.

As the whale descends, the air in its lungs is compressed. This does not involve a relatively large volume, however, because the whale's lungs are rather small in comparison to its overall size (one to three percent as contrasted to seven percent for humans). As the water pressure increases, the lungs collapse completely and air is squeezed into the airways, where no further exchange of air into the bloodstream can take place.

Nearly 80 percent of air is nitrogen, which does not pass out of the tissues and bloodstream as quickly as other gases do. Because a human diver breathes compressed air from tanks *underwater*, he takes in huge volumes of *compressed* nitrogen. If he ascends too rapidly, the nitrogen bubbles expand in his bloodstream, rupturing tissues, thus causing the "bends." But the whale takes in air on the surface, so the nitrogen bubbles in its bloodstream can expand only to their original size as the whale ascends. Thus the whale does not get the bends.

When the whale surfaces, the telltale blow shoots skyward in a plume of mist. Some scientists maintain that the warm breath of the whale simply condenses as it reaches the cooler atmosphere, but this does not explain blows in hot regions. Other researchers claim that some water is taken into the lungs under pressure. A few authorities say that when air squeezes past the nostrils, it is compressed and heats up. Once in the atmosphere, the pressure and heat would be reduced, causing the air to expand and cool, condensing into the familiar blow. But motor-driven cameras now reveal the

A blue whale surfaces to breathe. As it first emerges, the whale's blowholes—actually its nostrils—are clamped shut (left). Often the whale will begin to exhale when it is still barely underwater. On the surface, the blow becomes a geyser as water trapped in the recesses formed by the closed nostrils is suddenly vaporized by the force of exhalation (top). The sound of the blow and the escaping is almost explosive. Once the nostrils are clear and the whale has exhaled, it draws in a huge breath. At this point (right), the nostrils have popped up like a ramp, which shunts the seas away from the whale's blowholes so that it can breathe without swallowing any water.

answer—whales begin to exhale just beneath the surface, vaporizing the water.

Most whales breathe a few times after they surface, then dive again. Deep-diving animals like the sperm whale may take up to 60 breaths before returning to the depths. Old whalers called this "having his spoutings out."

When the dolphin dives, a similar process takes place. The dolphin's lungs are quite a bit larger in relation to its body. Thus, the animal can take in more oxygen, which probably enables it to chase down prey more efficiently because the power of its muscles is determined by how much oxygen they receive. Interestingly, the Dall porpoise, a very fast animal, holds three times more oxygen in its blood than does the slower bottlenosed dolphin. Moreover, the Dall has twice as much blood.

BEYOND THE FIVE SENSES

The sense of touch may also be linked to a cetacean's speed. A dolphin's skin hosts many cells sensitive to touch. These may automatically signal when the blubber should be wrinkled so that the animal's progress through the water will be streamlined with no conscious effort on its part. Also, nerve endings at the base of whiskers may serve as speedometers in many cetaceans, the vibrating hairs telegraphing the speed to the brain. (All cetaceans have whiskers—if not as adults, then at least during fetal development.) Cetaceans in general seem to be sensitive to touch, particularly during lovemaking—but they probably also enjoy a gentle rub or scratch.

Perhaps because the blubber layer beneath the skin is relatively insensitive to pain and cold, scientists once felt that touch was not an important sense to cetaceans. But the portion of the brain concerned with touch is significant and should not be discounted, particularly since cetaceans may not always use this sense in the same ways we do.

This is not true for smell, because cetaceans seem to have little need for it. The organs of smell have all but disappeared, and even the section of brain normally used for this sense is essentially undeveloped. But linked to smell is taste, and cetaceans probably do utilize this sense to some extent, if only to sample the water.

A Risso's dolphin blasts through the boundary between water and air like a missile launched from a submarine. No one is certain why dolphins and whales breach, leaping completely out of the water. In many cases, this may well be a display, either of aggression toward another animal, a way of establishing a territory, or even of impressing a prospective mate. It may also be a way of communication—certainly the resultant splash is very loud. Some researchers feel it may also be a way of knocking parasites off the animal's skin. This grizzled old veteran shows the scars of many a fracas with fellow dolphins and possibly with squid, its favorite prey.

Unlike the Risso's dolphin which normally is white or gray as an adult, this common dolphin is a rare albino. Common dolphins are usually gray and white, as seen in this albino's companion. This all-white individual lacks any skin pigment except for its scars. This particular animal was seen on several occasions over a two-year period and always seemed to be healthy. True albino cetaceans are quite rare. Most "albinos" turn out to be unusually light-colored specimens rather than true albinos.

A Dall porpoise explodes in a burst of spray. This animal is among the fastest of the small cetaceans, reaching bursts of speed in excess of 20 knots. It leaves a distinctive rooster tail of spray when it breaks the surface.

Blainville's whale, sometimes called the dense-beaked whale, is seldom seen. It probably spends much of its time far offshore. A few have been seen off Hawaii, but only two have been reported for the West Coast.

Cetaceans see well, but only for short distances, because even in the clearest water, visibility is not much better than it is during a thick fog on land. Moreover, the deeper the water becomes, the more the sunlight is filtered out. Even in extremely clear water, darkness is eternal beyond 1,500 feet or so.

To compensate for the darkness, cetaceans have *tapetums* in their eyes, mirror-like plates that flip up as the light grows dimmer, bouncing lost light back into the retina. The eyes themselves are shaped so the animals can see well underwater, but not above—the exact opposite of land mammals. The cornea is protected by a tough membrane. As might be expected, tear ducts are lacking—instead, a thin, oily substance lubricates the eyes.

Many creatures, especially large whales, cannot see straight ahead. Dolphins and some small toothed whales can, perhaps making it easier to chase down prey as they close in for the kill. But how do cetaceans initially locate their prey in a world of perpetual fog?

Sound travels several times faster underwater than it does on land. We can seldom hear creatures underwater because our ears are not adapted to the environment, but the silent world is anything but serene. Shrimp make noises, especially when they travel in large shoals. Fish are audible as they swim—some even call to one another. And when any creature breaks the surface, its presence is broadcast everywhere.

Cetaceans have evolved a unique way of hearing underwater. No external lobes funnel sounds to the eardrums—the lobes have been sacrificed for streamlining. The openings that lead to the eardrums are all but closed. Even on a large whale the orifices are no larger than a wooden match, and they are still more constricted farther in. Because of these anatomical features, scientists once felt that cetaceans were essentially deaf.

Actually, cetaceans hear rather well. The ear canals are blocked because water is almost the same density as the tissues of the animals—a water-filled canal would prevent them from discerning the direction of the sounds. (This is why we cannot interpret sound direction accurately underwater.) Bones conduct sound vibrations too, further confusing the signal. To compensate for these problems, the inner ear of cetaceans is filled with an oily foam which insulates each hearing mechanism from vibrations from the surrounding bones and tissues. The animals can easily distinguish the direction a sound is coming from because each hearing mechanism is acoustically isolated from the other.

When a cetacean dives, the water pressure against the ears is equalized by more oily bubbles squeezed in from surrounding cavities. Because the oil suspending the bubbles is virtually incompressible, the bubbles persist even under tremendous pressure, continuing to deflect unwanted vibrations from the hearing mechanism.

When baleen whales call to one another, they often use a very loud but low-frequency sound that can be discerned over considerable distances. Many toothed whales and dolphins emit sounds of a much higher frequency, however. These "clicks" are used to locate prey as well as to examine their surroundings. (The bat, another mammal that cannot use vision to locate

Bottlenose dolphins, popular in marine-life parks, are found throughout the tropical to subtemperate seas of much of the world. Two forms seem to exist, one sticking very close to shore, even to the point of traveling up rivers, the other staying well offshore in deep water.

The striped dolphin is perhaps among the most beautiful of dolphins. Seeing one flying through the air is a memorable experience.

Overleaf: The mighty flukes of a diving humpback attest to its tremendous strength. Photo by Deborah A. Glockner-Ferrari.

The spinner dolphin of warmer seas gets its name from its habit of spinning while in midair. Five forms have been described by scientists, who still argue over what to call each one.

This common dolphin is a study in fluid grace as it vaults from the sea in a graceful arch. Dolphins take advantage of waves at sea, planing along on their pectoral fins down the slope of a wave, then leaping out of the water for a breath before they lose momentum as the wave passes.

should remember what its brain is actually used for and attempt to interpret the information it processes. To try to speak to an intelligence geared chiefly toward utilizing a sense we do not even possess is like someone who has always been blind trying to tell us what sight is like. In fact, it is even more difficult, for not only are we unable to naturally produce the same vocal sounds, we can't even speak the language—if it can be called that.

Many animals are capable of vocalizing emotions. A dog yelping in pain, a dolphin squeaking in distress, a person screaming in terror—all express genuine emotions, yet none is speaking a language. A wolf can call to others in its pack, signaling its position and even its identity. So can a whale, but this is not a language either. A parrot can imitate a person's voice, but the parrot is far from being an intellectual giant.

True language is a demonstration of intelligence as we know it. When vocalizations can express past, present, and future, and when they can be phrased into new combinations to express rational thoughts, then they form a language. As far as we know, cetaceans do not do this.

Man's intelligence has developed through communication in the form of language. This has been essential to our very existence, because we are quite helpless until we learn to survive in our environment. Cetaceans, even at birth, have little need for language. They can swim almost immediately; they are protected and fed by others; and they can learn how to survive merely by example. This does not imply that they lack intelligence, but rather that it is foolish to measure their intelligence by our standards.

The northern right whale dolphin is distinguished by its lanky, streamlined form and lack of dorsal fin. Its extremely sleek shape allows it to travel very swiftly.

Dolphins, like all cetaceans, must learn to swim at birth. This spotted dolphin mother is very attentive toward her calf. She will coax it to the surface to breathe, then encourage it to swim. Within only weeks, it will be able to match its mother's speed.

A Pacific spotted dolphin forms an elegant silhouette. These animals were slaughtered only because they swam over tuna schools and were caught in nets. Although the toll from the American fleet was greatly reduced, vessels of other countries continue to kill all too many.

The Gentlest Carnivores

All cetaceans, gentle as they usually are, are carnivores. The great baleen whales feed by straining creatures from the water through their brushlike baleen plates, while toothed whales and dolphins snap up their prey.

Largely because of their dentition, cetaceans are divided into two scientific orders—the baleen whales, or *mysticetes,* and the toothed cetaceans, or *odontocetes.* Each order is broken down into several families. The breakdown is reasonably clear-cut from a scientific standpoint.

When common names are used, however, this tidy breakdown disintegrates. Some cetaceans are popularly called dolphins—others, porpoises. Authorities have contrived neat definitions to overcome this confusion, but exceptions to their rules only cloud the issue. A few dolphins are called whales, and certain whales are called dolphins. The most ambiguous name of all is the northern right whale dolphin.

Both dolphins and porpoises are small, toothed cetaceans. Whales are also cetaceans that have either teeth or baleen plates and usually exceed 14 feet in length. Three cetaceans are smaller than this, but are still called whales because they resemble larger species (pygmy sperm whales, dwarf sperm whales, and pygmy killer whales). The melon-headed whales, which grow to only seven and a half feet, would seem to be an exception, but they closely resemble the pygmy killer whales.

The Biters

Toothed cetaceans far outnumber baleen whales. The largest is no stranger to anyone who has read *Moby Dick*. Yet in many ways the sperm whale remains a mystery to us.

No one is certain why this animal has a huge, oil-filled forehead, but this has not stopped researchers from coming up with several fascinating explanations. One scientist maintains that the oil is used to absorb carbon dioxide. Another feels that the reservoir is used as a buoyancy tank. When the supply of warm blood to the cavity is cut down as the whale dives and cold water shoots down the left nasal passage—which runs through the cavity—the oil condenses, hardening into a

These melon-headed whales are readily identified, not so much by the shape of their heads as by their distinctive white "mustaches" and dark saddles under their dorsal fins. They are found worldwide in tropical and subtropical waters.

Largest of the toothed whales, a sperm whale glides through the depths. Males can reach over 50 feet in length and weigh over 40 tons; females stretch about 35 feet and weigh only 13 tons. These animals dive down over a mile in quest of such exotic prey as giant squid. Suction cup marks the size of dinner plates have been found on sperm whales, proof of Herculean battles far beyond the sight of humans. Usually the whales emerge victorious, perhaps because they apparently can project tremendous volumes of sound, stunning their prey.

This perpetually smiling Cuvier's beaked whale is rarely seen except by people who spend time way offshore, past where the continental shelf drops into the deeper reaches of the sea. This is the home of the Cuvier's beaked whale, where it dives to abysmal depths in search of its prey. This unusual animal has only two teeth, both on the tip of its lower jaw.

Few sights can be quite as daunting as that of a charging orca bull. These impressive animals possess a definite presence that proclaims beyond any doubt that they are the monarchs of their realm. Virtually no creatures would dare challenge their supremacy. In the face of such a menace, the best most creatures can do is to defend themselves as well as they can, which is not always well enough.

wax that is not as buoyant as the fluid. When the blood returns, the oil supposedly expands into a buoyant liquid again.

Another theory suggests that the oil-filled chamber conducts sounds produced in one of the nasal passages. These sounds are then reflected off the curved shape of the front of the skull—colorfully dubbed Neptune's Chariot by early Yankee whalers—and beamed forward.

The sperm whale probably does echolocate its prey, for it sometimes hunts in abysmal blackness, grappling with giant squid thousands of feet down. It eats small squid as well.

Sperm whales, along with dolphins and other toothed whales, may even stun their prey by beaming tremendous volumes of sound at them. Several times, fish have been observed swimming erratically, in a confused manner, just before they were gobbled up by echolocating cetaceans. Even though cetaceans sometimes do produce an incredible magnitude of sound, other scientists feel that cetaceans may simply chase their prey until it tires, then gulp it down.

Killer whales, now usually called orcas, are something of a paradox. In captivity they are often surprisingly gentle and cooperative. But in the wild they are supreme predators, capable of devouring seals, sea lions, walruses, and dolphins. They even prey on the great whales. Their awesome abilities have earned them a formidable reputation. Like most top-level predators, however, killers cull out the weakest and slowest of large prey. Some groups actually rely upon fish and squid for the bulk of their diet. Transient groups seem to seek out marine mammals to prey upon.

Orcas track their prey by a variety of methods. Their hearing is acute, while their echolocating abilities are finely tuned. Like other odontocetes, they may stun their prey with sound. Finally, unlike all other cetaceans, orcas poke their head out of the water to look for prey, spotting seals sprawled on ice cakes and rocks.

Orcas hunt in packs like wolves when a larger quarry appears. They apparently wear down or cripple their prey by clamping onto its flippers or tail. They push their quarry hard, trying to prevent it from surfacing to breathe so it will soon become exhausted. Despite such coordinated attacks, large whales often escape. Fearsome scars remain as evidence of such encounters.

Although dolphins—even wild ones—are renowned for their friendly demeanor, they are also quite ruthless and efficient predators. Small schooling fish and squid make up the preferred diet of most dolphins, although a few eat shrimplike crustaceans as well. Like other toothed cetaceans, dolphins echolocate their prey and perhaps even immobilize it with sound beams.

In a display of power, an orca leaps out of the water. The bright white markings, contrasted against the jet black and coupled with the size, make orcas unmistakable. Males, which reach some 30 feet in length and weigh up to 8 tons, dwarf the females, which only grow to about 22 feet and 4 tons.

This gray whale has had a close call with orcas. Note the evenly spaced, white scars on its lower fluke, the telltale teeth marks of an adult orca. A surprising number of gray whales have been marked by orcas. Apparently many attacks are not successful.

Humpback whales sometimes feed by circling schools of fish or krill to get them to mill around in a tight circle, then lunging upwards through the prey with open mouths, swallowing hundreds of creatures in a single gulp. Gulls attracted by the frenzied prey often try to partake in the spoils of such a feast, occasionally to be accidentally engulfed themselves. This gull made a very narrow escape.

The Gulpers and Skimmers

Although small schooling fish are an important part of the diet of many whales, *krill*, consisting of shrimplike creatures smaller than your little finger, is the staff of life for some species. Krill abounds in polar waters. Sometimes it is so thick the sea turns red.

Swimming through this living stew are the great whales. The rorquals, including blue, fin, sei, Bryde's (pronounced "BREW-ders") and minke whales, eat by gulping a mouthful of water, then forcefully expelling it with their huge tongue. Humpbacks feed in the same manner. This volume of water is augmented when the pleatlike longitudinal grooves under the chin and along the throat are expanded, much like the bellows of a concertina. This enables a large blue whale to take in up to 70 tons of water at a gulp.

As the water is forcefully expelled by the tongue, perhaps assisted by the throat muscles, the krill is strained out in the baleen plates, then swallowed. Baleen, like our fingernails and hair, is made from keratin. Baleen plates do not replace the teeth that disappear during fetal development—instead, they seem to emerge as extensions of the transverse ridges of the palate. The rorquals and humpbacks have short baleen plates that completely encircle the mouth, making efficient food strainers.

Some rorquals feed on their side near the surface, perhaps so they can turn quickly to encircle fast preylike fish. The fin whale feeds on its right side, which is white around the mouth—its other side is dark. White is more difficult to see from below, whereas black is harder to spot from above. This uneven coloring could serve two purposes—the bold markings could frighten fish toward the whale's mouth, and the color patterns could make it difficult to see the mouth itself.

Humpbacks often "lobtail," crashing their flukes down on the surface with a loud noise. Like breaching, this probably is a display to other whales.

The right side of the fin whale's mouth is white, while the left is gray.

The largest predators on earth eat some of the smallest creatures. It takes a lot of krill to fill even a human hand.

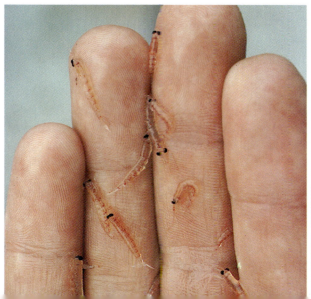

Some whales slap their fins on the surface as they circle their prey, perhaps to herd them into a tight ball. The humpback blows a ring of bubbles around a school of fish, causing the fish to mill about in a confused circle, then surfaces in their midst, engulfing thousands in its cavernous mouth.

Gulping is a very efficient means of feeding. A blue whale can devour up to four tons of krill a day, or 8 million tiny animals. The fin whale eats up to three tons, but the sei manages only a ton and a half.

Sei whales obtain their food by skimming the surface with their mouth open as well as

Belugas, or white whales, inhabit the frozen waters of the Arctic. The white pigmentation probably helps them blend in with the ice and snow. Occasionally, belugas become stranded on the ice. When this occurs, they remain perfectly still until high tide returns, otherwise they could be spotted by polar bears, which will eat them. Belugas are highly vocal animals with an impressive repertoire of chirps, squeaks, and whistles. Although they thrive in very cold water, they can tolerate surprisingly high temperatures when they venture up rivers. For this reason, belugas can be kept in captivity in relatively warm water.

FLIP NICKLIN / MINDEN PICTURES

by gulping. But right whales are the true specialists in the art of skimming. Their baleen plates are quite long—up to 14 feet as compared to 3 or 4 feet for the rorquals. Moreover, the baleen of the right whale does not completely encircle the mouth. Instead, a gap in front allows water to rush into the mouth as the whale slowly swims along. Right whales lack pleated throat grooves, but since they feed by skimming, they don't really need them. Every so often the whale closes its mouth and swallows the krill trapped in the fine strands of baleen.

Although gray whales also feed by skimming, they are primarily bottom feeders. Grays usually plow a furrow along the sand or mud of the sea floor, straining out organisms that live there. They feed on their right side, which is often scraped nearly clean of barnacles around the mouth. The baleen on this side is shortened because it is used more.

Baleen whales, especially humpbacks, emit an intriguing variety of sounds. No evidence has yet been discovered proving they can echolocate.

THE LONGEST SWIM

Every year the gray whale migrates 6,000 or 7,000 miles down the west coast, from the Bering Sea to Baja California, then returns. Once believed to be the longest migration of any mammal, it is actually bettered by the right whale of the Atlantic coast. The gray whale usually swims across long-established corridors, however, making its yearly movements highly predictable.

How does the gray whale navigate over such a vast distance if it does not use echolocation? No one really knows, although several explanations are possible. Some observers believe that the gray whale may find its way by rearing its head out of the water to spot

Authorities once believed that gray whales formed mating trios—one male would help support the female in the water as the other male mated with her. Lately an entirely new concept has emerged. Scientists now believe that the male that penetrates the deepest and delivers the most sperm displaces the sperm from other males, thus he sires the calf. This odd reproductive strategy, called sperm competition, apparently is found in a few other whales as well as in some other animals. Here, an aroused male approaches the female as another male leaves. Although much of the mating takes place in the lagoons of Baja California, some mating does take place on the migration itself.

landmarks. But most whales are notoriously nearsighted, especially out of the water. Besides, how could they obtain bearings on foggy days? Perhaps they simply follow the contours of the coast and of the sea floor, keeping the rising sun on their left on their way down, spurred by the vanguard of animals ahead of them. Possibly they learn the route by following others, later passing on their knowledge to new generations.

At any rate, in late fall the pregnant females head south, followed by the other females, and finally by the males. They travel in loosely knit groups of up to 16 animals, often cutting corners rather than hugging the coast. They eat little or nothing on the way.

Winter finds the grays congregated in the warm, protected lagoons of Baja California. As each calf is born, it is often helped to the surface by its mother, for its flippers usually emerge curled up from nearly 13 months of

The Bryde's whale is readily identified by three ridges that extend forward of the blowhole to the snout. No other baleen whale has these characteristics. The Bryde's whale inhabits tropical and subtropical waters on both sides of America.

confinement in the womb. The calf swims quite well within just a few hours of its birth, however.

A newborn calf is about a third the length of its mother—more than 12 feet—and weighs over a ton. It doesn't have a rich blubber layer at birth, so warm water is essential for the nursery ground.

The calf gains weight very quickly because whale milk has ten times the fat content of cow milk. It nurses by nuzzling its mother's recessed nipples until she squirts a jet of milk into its mouth. The calf stays very close to its mother, who jealously protects it from all comers, orcas and sharks included. The calf nurses at least seven months, if not closer to a year.

Mature females breed every other year because they will not accept a male's advances when they are nursing. Since half the overall population is male, each barren female is usually accompanied by more than one bull.

By March the gray whales leave the lagoons, heading north to their summer feeding grounds. They stay quite close to shore on the way back, often venturing into kelp beds, sometimes to strain out the bugs that live on the leaves. Otherwise they eat little, living mostly on stored fat. Gray whales can lose up to nearly 30 percent of their overall weight during migration.

The young calves are vulnerable to orcas' attacks during their journey northward. This may explain why grays frequent the kelp beds. They would be harder to see there. They would also be harder to echolocate, because the gas-filled bulbs on kelp leaves reflect sonar signals.

Some grays, especially young ones, do not go all the way to the Bering Sea. Instead, they summer at several food-rich areas along the coast from California to British Columbia. These younger animals may linger in southern waters because the freezing polar seas may simply be too cold for them—at least until they can build up a thick layer of blubber. The young animals expose far more of their surface area in relation to their overall body size than larger whales do, and water dissipates heat 25 times faster than air. Paradoxically, whales need a great deal of food to stay warm, yet the largest concentrations of food are found in the icy waters of the north.

Sei whales are found throughout the temperate and subtemperate waters of both the Pacific and Atlantic sides of America. Although they are predominantly gray, they are spotted with oval scars inflicted by a parasitic tropical fish called the lamprey.

Other baleen whales migrate, but not as far, nor over such defined routes. Then too, they do not calve and breed in shallow lagoons, although nearly all of them do frequent polar seas during the summer months. Most whales seem to feed day and night while in the polar grounds, heading south only when threatened by the advance of the ice.

Bowhead whales are the least migratory of all baleen whales and inhabit polar seas year-round. They can even break through thin ice or lift it up to breathe. Conversely, Bryde's whales stay in warmer water throughout the year, thriving on fish and plankton.

Sperm whales tend to drift away from the tropics during the summer, some bulls reaching as far as the polar regions, but they have no distinct migrational paths. Orcas are the most widely distributed of all cetaceans, ranging from the ice floes of both poles to the equator. Some populations, however, remain in their own territories.

Other toothed whales and dolphins seem to follow their prey throughout the year. Because water temperatures fluctuate from year to year, the distribution of these cetaceans is sporadic on the edges of their ranges, but it is fairly predictable in their familiar haunts.

The southern right whale is often encountered off the Patagonian coast of South America. Right whales were so named because they were slow, easy to kill, and floated when dead—they were the "right" whales.

This stranded minke, sometimes called little piked whale, is the smallest of the baleen whales. It feeds on small fish, squid, and krill.

Humans and Cetaceans

Almost always, every natural resource necessary for human survival can be found in a given area. It takes perseverance, ingenuity, and a high degree of adaptability to ferret out such resources and thrive upon them, especially in hostile climes.

In the frozen lands of the north, people must metabolize large quantities of fat to stay warm. This requires a substantial intake of rich meat. If they are to build anything on the treeless tundra, they must have materials. And finally, they must have light to brighten the insane darkness of the polar winters. The whale can provide all this—and more.

It is not surprising that the Eskimo people have relied upon whales as an important part of their subsistence for more than 3,500 years. The whale provided them with bones for framing huts, sleds, and boats when wood was not available. The baleen was bent into different shapes for a variety of purposes or was shredded into thongs for lashings. The gut was dried and cut into thongs, too.

Sometimes the entrails were pickled for food stores—they prevented scurvy. The meat and blubber were shared by the inhabitants of each village. Preserving food for the long winters was seldom a problem—the inhospitable environment of ice and snow actually helped those who strove to live there. The Eskimo hunters rendered much of the blubber into oil rather than freezing it. The oil was kept in seal skins and used for lamp fuel or for trading with inland tribes.

Today the Eskimo are still allowed to hunt cetaceans, taking only what is necessary for their own subsistence. But many use modern implements including bomb lances, snowmobiles, and outboard motors. This has generated a controversy between native whalers and conservationists, who maintain that the hunt is no longer a traditional one.

The bowhead whale is the most endangered of all species. Only a few thousand survive, even though the Eskimo feel that plenty of them still exist. Until an accurate bowhead census has been taken, it will be difficult to further restrict Eskimo whaling activities. Certainly they should be allowed to follow their old ways, but not at the expense of jeopardizing the very existence of the bowhead.

Other North American natives also hunted whales, although they do not today. The Aleut harpooned whales with spears dipped in aconite, a deadly poison. The lances were notched so they would break off and work their way into the whale's vitals as it struggled. Indians of the Pacific Northwest were particularly accomplished whalers, pursuing their prey in long dugout canoes.

These natives of North America took only what they needed to survive. They probably helped the overall whale population by culling out weak, slow, and less intelligent individuals.

Kayaks, designed by the Eskimo people for hunting marine mammals, are usually a great way to view whales and dolphins, provided one maintains a respectful distance. This kayaker accidentally ended up too close to the humpback whale, spooking it as it surfaced. His camera was soaked.

The bowhead whale inhabits the chilly waters of the Arctic. It can reach up to 60 feet in length and weigh an incredible 100 tons, only slightly less than a really big blue whale weighs. The tip of its lower jaw is white, sometimes with black spots. Its baleen can stretch up to 9 feet, earning it the scientific name of "mustache whale."

The size of a blue whale is difficult to imagine. It is the largest creature ever found on this planet. Compared to the whale, the dolphins seem tiny, yet the human is even smaller. The blue whale can eat up to four tons of food a day, but like most larger whales, it is usually gentle. In fact it is more like a grazing animal in many ways, although it can be formidable when aroused.

The Whalers

Tragically, Caucasians were the ones who slaughtered whales in droves—not to feed struggling villagers, but to fill the coffers of a greedy few. As technology improved, even the fastest and most intelligent whales were unable to escape. Most were hunted until it was no longer economically feasible to pursue them. In many cases this meant they were perilously close to extinction. The Atlantic gray whale was hunted to extinction a few centuries ago.

In the 1880s the whaling industry provided products similar to those supplied by the petroleum industry of today. Whale blubber yielded oil for lighting and lubrication. Baleen, or whalebone as it was called, was widely used as a tough, flexible material replaced today by plastics. Flesh and bone were used as fertilizer or animal food. Teeth were carved into trinkets.

In the Old Country, whalers had chased their quarry just offshore in long, fast rowing craft, throwing a harpoon into them at point-blank range. Although this was not much more efficient than the Native American techniques, more whales were killed because they were sought for profit rather than for survival. All too soon, whalers of many nations were journeying to the remotest parts of the globe in sailing ships, processing their catch on board instead of towing it to shore. Right whales—so called because they were slow, easy to kill, and floated when dead—were decimated, and later, the bowheads.

In 1857, Yankee whaler Charles Melville Scammon picked his way through the treacherous entrance of a lagoon in Baja California and found gray whales "in countless numbers about us." The grays, too, were soon annihilated, and in just a few decades it was no longer profitable to hunt them.

Steam outmoded sail, steel supplanted wood, and an exploding harpoon, fired from a deck gun, replaced the hand-thrown spears and bomb lances. An accumulator, which acted like a shock absorber, eased the tremendous strain on harpoon lines. Hollow lances enabled whalers to inflate their victims so that even the heaviest rorquals would float. Huge, sophisticated factory ships increased the whaling fleet's range and capacity. The slaughter intensified.

MICHIO HOSHINO / MINDEN PICTURES

Products that eliminated our dependency on whales, followed eventually by an enlightened attitude toward the conservation of our living resources, finally tipped the balance back. Grays on the west coast, once close to extinction, have made a remarkable recovery and probably are as numerous now as they were before the days of commercial whaling.

Other species have not been so fortunate. Several rorquals, the humpback, and the sperm whale are still considered endangered. Some species, including the blue whale, may never recover. And the Atlantic gray whale is extinct.

Dolphins have fared better. Too small to be of much commercial value, they were never seriously exploited by modern whalers. Many dolphins were swept up in fishing nets and drowned only because they followed vast tuna and salmon schools. Improved techniques and modified nets, in addition to the diligence of National Marine Fisheries Service observers, have substantially cut the toll in the last few years. Fishing practices of other nations remain a problem, however.

Today the National Marine Fisheries Service, under the U.S. Department of Commerce, is responsible for managing most marine mammal stocks in American waters. The Marine Mammal Protection Act of 1972 established a moratorium on the taking of any marine mammal without a special permit issued by the Fisheries Service. Whales may be hunted for subsistence purposes only by the Eskimo. Some cetaceans, seals, and sea lions

The gray whale (left) sometimes ventures into the ice, occasionally to be trapped when the leads in the ice freeze over. Eskimo people from both Siberia and Alaska still eat gray whales, although bowheads are favored. The natives also eat narwhals (above). Sadly, many narwhals were killed for their tusks, which are actually elongated teeth. Narwhals only have two teeth. Usually the left tooth of the male grows outward in a spiral, eventually reaching a length of over nine feet. Occasionally, females grow tusks, too, but this is exceptional.

Orcas in captivity have proved to be surprisingly gentle creatures. Their patience has limits, however, and savvy trainers are quick to pick up on this. The whales subtly—and not so subtly—telegraph their reluctance to undergo training when they are not in the mood. All acts involving marine mammals rely upon the animals' interest in food. Most of the shows simply take advantage of a creature's normal behavior, such as jumping or opening its mouth. These habits are forged into a routine, often with some kind of theme.

Fraser's dolphins inhabit the tropical regions of both the Atlantic and Pacific coasts. They are pelagic—that is, they wander endlessly in search of food. Fraser's dolphins, like other oceanic dolphins, are the vagabonds of the sea. Since their usual haunts are well offshore, they are rarely seen. Some have turned up as mortalities in tuna fishing nets, although the American catch of such animals has dwindled considerably, thanks to activists who saw to it that the American fleet obeyed the law.

are allowed to be caught incidentally by fishermen, but only under strict guidelines. A few cetaceans may be collected by scientists for research purposes or by oceanariums for public display. The Marine Mammal Protection Act has finally provided the federal government with the power it needed to protect cetaceans.

The Catchers

After dolphins were captured for Marineland of the Pacific in 1954, the appeal of cetaceans to the public was quickly recognized. Other species were soon captured.

The smaller cetaceans were usually snared in long-handled hoop nets as each animal surfaced to breathe just ahead of the bow of a catch boat. As the animal hit the strands, the net unraveled from the hoop like a sock. A 100- or 200-fathom line with a buoy on the end was then played out to tire the struggling animal. Some dolphins were captured with a tail-grab, a padded, clawlike device that clamped shut on impact. Orcas were pinched off with gill nets in the narrow channels of the Pacific Northwest. They proved to be surprisingly gentle in captivity. Having such creatures in areas where they can be closely studied has greatly increased our knowledge of cetaceans.

Various Native American tribes hunted cetaceans, while others may have revered them as deities. Being careful not to touch the rock, a researcher at the Channel Islands off southern California points to a pictograph or cave painting of dolphins. Such paintings are usually made with natural pigments. Some are hundreds of years old.

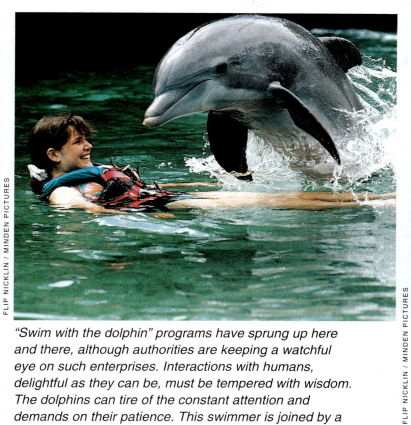

"Swim with the dolphin" programs have sprung up here and there, although authorities are keeping a watchful eye on such enterprises. Interactions with humans, delightful as they can be, must be tempered with wisdom. The dolphins can tire of the constant attention and demands on their patience. This swimmer is joined by a bottlenose dolphin that seems happy at the chance of jumping over a new hurdle.

Nothing compares to diving into the open ocean with a great whale. The size, grace, and restrained power of such giants is truly awesome. By entering the whale's world, researchers are able to glean valuable information about the lives of these leviathans. Here, a diver is dwarfed by a humpback whale.

The rough-toothed dolphin has a pointed snout that tapers gently into the head region, giving it something of a sharklike profile. This animal frequents the tropical and warm temperate waters of much of the earth, staying well offshore.

Persons visiting Puget Sound, in Washington state, or the Inland Passage that winds through British Columbia and southeast Alaska, are likely to see pods of orcas. These particular groups, many of which live there year-round, are the best known of all the wild orca populations. They are not shy of boats that share the waterways with the huge predators.

THE WHALEWATCHERS

Cetaceans may readily perceive the intentions of humans in boats. Anything that suggests a threat usually makes them wary. A gradual, gentle approach often does not alarm them, however. Sometimes they will swim alongside a boat, or even rub against the hull.

Such trusting behavior has allowed a multi-million-dollar business to blossom—and all that people do is watch whales. But some scientists feel even this could have adverse effects, particularly when the watchers press for too close a look and frighten the animals. In time, whales might begin to avoid areas where they have been continually pestered on previous occasions. Migrating gray whales may already be following new paths because of harassment, at least according to some authorities.

SUGGESTED READING

ELLIS, RICHARD. *The Book of Whales.* New York: Alfred Knopf, 1980.

ELLIS, RICHARD. *Men and Whales.* New York: Albert A. Knopf, 1993.

LEATHERWOOD, STEPHEN and RANDALL R. REEVES. *The Sierra Club Handbook of Whales.* San Francisco: The Sierra Club, 1983.

NICKLIN, FLIP. *With the Whales.* Minocqua, Wisconsin: NorthWord Press, Inc., 1990.

WATSON, LYLE. *The Sea Guide to Whales of the World.* New York: E. P. Dutton, 1981.

Occasionally, individual whales take a liking to a boat and show only curiosity toward people. This particular humpback could easily leave if it chose; instead, it seems to prefer hanging around the boat.

Another way of watching whales and dolphins is in the water. No swimmer can begin to match the speed and agility of a dolphin, which can rocket out of sight in a heartbeat if it chooses. In some areas, dolphins seem to be curious and trusting toward humans. Considering our history toward animals, this is remarkable. Let us hope that we continue to merit their trust.

A sperm whale has fallen victim to a fishing net. Unless rescued, this animal will slowly die of exhaustion from dragging the heavy net around, or from starvation, since stalking and catching prey would be difficult. Drift nets and gill nets are still used in many parts of the world. In some regions, such entanglements are rare—in others, catastrophic.

Overleaf: *A short-finned pilot whale glides majestically through the deep blue sea. Photo by James D. Watt.*

Cetaceans and the Future

Simple economics often dictate a country's actions far more than any qualities we esteem in humans. Had it not been for the burgeoning of the petroleum industry at a time when stocks of whales were dwindling, several species might have been hunted to extinction. Conservation efforts made by the International Whaling Commission on behalf of each species did not begin until hunting a particular type of whale was no longer profitable. It is encouraging that watching whales is now more lucrative than killing them.

Unfortunately, this outlook is not shared by some countries which continue to hunt whales. They see cetaceans as a harvestable resource, another commodity to market. In Russia some of the meat is given to the Siberian Eskimo, but all too much of it is used for food on mink farms. The Japanese continue to eat whale meat obtained for "research" purposes, although political pressure from the United States, plus a growing trend toward boycotting Japanese goods, may turn the tide. Norway and Iceland resumed hunting minke whales in 1993. A few Third World countries, together with "pirate" whalers, also hunt cetaceans, although opposition is steadily mounting toward them.

Certainly the greatest resources we have on this planet are the living ones, because they can replenish themselves, thus ensuring their own future. But whenever we take a hand in exploiting them, we should be responsible for preserving them. Our finest legacy could well be the salvation of the largest and one of the most intelligent creatures the world has ever known.

A southern right whale mother is very attentive toward its calf.

Inside back cover: A lone kayaker enjoys a magic moment with two Risso's dolphins. Photo by Peter C. Howorth.

Back cover: A smiling coastal bottlenose dolphin greets the reflections of its admirers. Photo by Peter C. Howorth.

Other books on marine life: Big Sur, Biscayne, Channel Islands, Santa Catalina Island, Sharks. By publishers of "The Story Behind the Scenery" and "in pictures...The Continuing Story" books on national park areas. Selected titles in both series are available with French, German, or Japanese translations bound into the center of the English book. To receive our catalog listing over 90 titles call: 1-800-626-9673, fax: 702-433-3420, or write to the address below:

KC Publications, 3245 E. Patrick Ln., Suite A, Las Vegas, NV 89120.

Created, Designed and Published in the U.S.A.
Printed by Dong-A Printing and Publishing, Seoul, Korea
Color Separations by Kedia/Kwangyangsa Co., Ltd.

Salem: A Pictorial History of Oregon's Capital is sponsored by Commercial Bank for the benefit of A. C. Gilbert's Discovery Village. This special publication is dedicated to the community and its children.

THE
DONNING COMPANY
PUBLISHERS

Expanded Edition
Including 1980–1998

by Harry H. Stein

Salem
A Pictorial History of Oregon's Capital

To my daughter, Serena

Copyright © 1981, 1998 by Harry H. Stein

All rights reserved, including the right to reproduce this book in any form whatsoever without permission in writing from the publisher, except for brief passages in connection with a review. For information, write:
        The Donning Company/Publishers
        184 Business park Drive, Suite 106
        Virginia Beach, VA 23462-6533

First Edition 1981
        Jacqueline Lane, Pictorial Marketing Director
        Donna Reiss Friedman, Editor
        Jamie Backus Raynor, Graphic Designer

Expanded Second Edition 1998
        Steve Mull, General Manager
        Barbara A. Bolton, Project Director
        Dawn V. Kofroth, Assistant General Manager
        Richard A. Horwege, Senior Editor
        Paul C. Gualdoni, Jr., Graphic Designer
        James Casper, Imaging Artist
        Teri S. Arnold, Senior Marketing Coordinator

Library of Congress Cataloging in Publication Data

Stein, Harry H., 1938–
        Salem, a pictorial history of Oregon's capital.
        1. Salem, Or.—Description—Views.
        2. Salem, Or.—History—Pictorial works. I. Title
F884.S2S8   978.5'37   80-27805
ISBN 1-57864-045-8 (exp. second edit.)   AACR1

Printed in the United States of America

Contents

Foreword 6

Preface 9

Chapter One
      1840–1880 .10

Chapter Two
      1880–1900 .28

Chapter Three
      1900–1920 .58

Chapter Four
      1920–1940 .104

Chapter Five
      1940–1960 .124

Chapter Six
      1960–1980 .154

Chapter Seven
      1980–1998 .190

Afterword 205

Sources 205

Index 206

Foreword

Salem is the capital of Oregon, a county seat, and a center for state institutions and for education and industry. A good home for its 89,000 citizens, it is also a popular place to visit.

This sensitive work is Salem's first pictorial history. Harry Stein made an exhaustive survey of some 20,000 images of Salem from early times to almost yesterday. His selection documents Salem's traditions and changes, its people, institutions, and events. He reveals well-known and little-known historical aspects. His view of Salem is personal, thoughtful, and stimulating.

Early views of Salem are rarely available to anyone, unfortunately. The first daguerreotypes were mainly portraits. Fire destroying Salem's first photographic studio in 1880 lost much of the town's early record. So we have no representation of the State House burned in 1855 and no closeup of the first County Court House. After 1880 many views and scenes exist. Someday other early pictures may be found in attics, trunks or closets to enrich the early story of Salem.

Salem began as Jason Lee's Willamette Methodist Mission, and the Methodist church significantly shaped the town. The Indians, whom Methodists came to serve, were already a dying group and soon became migrants camping along town fringes. Rarely welcome, Blacks came with the first settlers but were never numerous. Immigrants did come from abroad: Germans, Swiss, Irish, Chinese and Koreans in the nineteenth century; Japanese, East Europeans, Hispanics and now Laotians in this one. These immigrants included Catholics and small numbers of Jews who enriched Protestant Salem. Early and late, though, Salem remained unusually homogenous—overwhelmingly white and native-born.

Since the nineteenth century struggle between Piety and Gaiety Hills, Salem encompassed more than one point of view. Willamette University, almost from the beginning, educated local leaders and gave cultural direction to the town. Non-Methodist leaders found schooling elsewhere. Sacred Heart, the first private school, has long offered still another educational option as do recent additions, Chemeketa Community College and Western Baptist College.

The location of Salem in the lush central Willamette Valley, where the river breaks through the Salem Hills from the south, was its great strength. The missionaries and the commercial mills alike profited from logs they floated in by river. Water power and river transportation made early Salem thrive. Better transportation was critical to its later development. Salem began with the Mission Mills and grew with the woolen and flouring mills, the iron works and lumber plants, then with printing, paper, and other healthy manufacturing enterprises.

Its location helped make Salem a regional center. In one of the nation's best agricultural sections, the town prospered by making agricultural machinery and by selling, processing, and shipping agricultural products to market. Improved river, road, rail, and air service has transformed Salem from a shopping place for the vicinity into the mid-Willamette Valley's main shopping center.

Local residents, up to World War I, traditionally owned and operated its major businesses and industries. Professional and mercantile groups led Salem during most of its history. Consolidation and national investment, first in chain stores and then through mergers, have taken much of the economic control outside Salem in recent years. Neighborhood groups currently train future leaders.

The town successfully fought to be made the capital, first of the territory, then of the state. It battled to gain and guard its investment in many state institutions and especially against the straying of agencies to Portland. State government, its buying power and employee force, has been a major factor in Salem's existence. Yet, state political leaders rarely were part of its development or cultural life. They came from elsewhere and were interested in statewide, not local matters. The federal government remained, except in wartime, a distant, nebulous influence on Salem until federal power grew in this century.

This book well illustrates these and many other topics, including families, homes and entertainment. About 300 images omit single portraits, but not individuals. As a pictorial history, it should help Salem realize its visual past and suggest to it new visual essays. The book is worthy of study and should inspire future documentation and interpretation of Salem.

DAVID DUNIWAY

Preface

I have tried to present Salem's history as individuals experienced it from first settlement days to the present. The pictures I have used try to outline significant dimensions of Salem and to lay out the rich texture of its people's lives. Finding some 20,000 images, I still faced gaps in its pictorial record since many important historical events and aspects were not captured on film or saved. Although I have used words for captions and introductions, I show Salem here as others have viewed it—with a camera.

These pictures are documents which will be useful when someone writes a full-scale history of Salem. That work should be done not only for the sake of Salem but also for an Oregon proud of its capital and a nation knowing too little of any state capital. Today, only scattered accounts and publications offer bits and pieces of Salem history. That history may be sought in the invaluable collections of the Oregon State Library, Salem Public Library, Oregon Historical Society, Oregon State Archives, and in other archives and libraries. Material evidence of its past exists in Salem buildings, artifacts, and other human creations. Further evidence is in the files of institutions and individuals and in the memories of people.

Numerous individuals have generously helped me in my search to recapture Salem's history in pictorial form. David Duniway heads the list. He has lavished both friendship and an unparalleled knowledge of Salem on me. Dr. Mark Beach and Kathleen Ryan, my co-authors for *Portland: A Pictorial History*, encouraged this Salem book at every stage, improved the final manuscript, and printed most of the photographs. Their intelligence and friendship continue to grace my life. Joan Glassel superbly typed the manuscript. I enjoyed unstinting aid from the excellent staffs of the Oregon State Library, particularly Glenn Hartwell and Betty Book; the Salem Public Library, where the Ben Maxwell and Hugh Morrow collections are Salem treasures; and the Oregon Historical Society, especially its photography department. Also, Dr. Edward Bassett kindly opened the files of the *Statesman-Journal*, and its library and reporting staff answered numerous questions. Al Jones, president of the Marion County Historical Society, warmly gave access to his photograph collection and offered helpful information. Mr. and Mrs. N. Morrell Crary freely opened the photographic files of McEwan Photo Shops and answered many questions. Ed Culp generously allowed me access to his own collection.

For sharing photographs and information, I also deeply appreciate the time and the willingness of Linda Berman; Mr. and Mrs. Evan Boise; Boise Cascade Paper Group, Salem, Oregon; Bush House; Donald L. Barrick; Castle and Cooke Foods; Chemeketa Community College; Emma Cherry; The City of Salem; The Commonwealth Fund; Frank D. Cross; Frances Duniway; Fairview Training Center; Friends of Deepwood; Hamman Stage Lines; Frank Hrubetz; Jason Lee Manor; Ernest Kapphahn; Professor John McManus; Marion County Clerk's Office; Marion County Health Department; Mary Minto; Mission Mill Museum Association; Oregon Department of Transportation; Oregon School for the Blind; Oregon State Archives; Oregon State Fair; Oregon State School for the Deaf; Oregon State Hospital; Elisabeth W. Potter; Carlisle B. Roberts; Salem Area Chamber of Commerce; Salem Art Association; Salem Department of Public Works; Salem Hospital; State Farm Insurance Company; Shirley Steeves; United States Bank of Oregon, Ladd and Bush Salem Branch; University of Oregon Library; John L. Wilkerson; and Willamette University.

Chapter One

In 1873 a coach, probably for Chemeketa House rail passengers, stood before the shaded, brick Tioga Block at State Street between Liberty and Commercial streets (now the Capitol Tower). To the right were the Patton Block and the Griswold Block containing Oregon's first J. K. Gill bookstore. With the Ladd and Bush Bank across the Street, they composed the town's best commercial properties. Photograph by James G. Crawford, courtesy of Oregon State Library

1840–1880

The Capitol around 1885. This was Salem's most important building from 1876 until the 1935 fire. Columns, rear and front porticoes, and a dome were added later to make it resemble the national capitol. The fence kept out stray horses and cattle. Courtesy of Mr. and Mrs. Evan Boise

"Chief" Quinaby of the Chemeketa Indians lived on handouts as a minor town character until he died in 1878. After the 1840s few native Americans were seen in Salem, except for occasional migrants camping beside Mill Creek, along the river, or in Marion Square, or showing up in finery for a church marriage. Courtesy of Oregon State Library

Salem sprang from the Reverend Jason Lee's need for new quarters in the Oregon Country. Lee and his followers had converted few native Americans to Methodism during their six years at Mission Bottom near the present Wheatland Ferry. Consequently, they moved south in 1840 to a water power site where Mill Creek nears the Willamette River. Here, they built a combined sawmill-gristmill and in 1841 a house and parsonage. Soon, they abandoned hope of converting the Kalapooian tribal clans and turned to educating settlers' children. They sold town lots to support their school, the forerunner of Willamette University. In 1846 naval lieutenant Neil Howison of the *Shark* considered their village "too little to be worthy an attempt at description."

Choice, chance, and ultimately great effort favored what Oregonians variously called Chemeketa, the Mill, the Institute, and finally Salem—anglicized from the Hebrew for "peace." It lay amid excellent farmland uncontested by native Americans. The river provided vital trade and communication routes, used first by keelboats and batteaux. However, it also meant floods and mosquitoes.

Settlers roughing out a few roads brought to Salem stagecoaches which provided access through passes to places beyond the hills and mountains. The village of fewer than a hundred people survived the rush to the California gold fields in 1849, gaining wealth which its men brought back. It soon got a fresh infusion of settlers. After the 1850s, California orders for Oregon produce and timber translated into continuing profits for Salem and other towns. Salem wheat, flour, and other products went into west coast and foreign commerce by steamboats. By 1853 robbers could seize a fortune of $5,000 in coin and gold dust in one Salem store.

Becoming the territorial, then the permanent state capital assured and stabilized Salem's future. However, this required fifteen years competition with other towns. At first, the governor and some judges refused to shift from Oregon City in 1851. In 1855, the legislature left briefly for

Corvallis then returned to Salem, where an arsonist immediately burned the new, unused State House. Arguments and elections over its retaining the capital continued after statehood in 1859, finally being decided for Salem in 1864. By securing the penitentiary and other state institutions in the 1860s the town furthered its importance and economy. Local church folk for years disdained the legislators and lobbyists who gathered biennially, considering them overly-crude and often corrupt. By the 1870s, government in its state, county, and local forms was Salem's big business. Finally a massive new Capitol building in 1876 signified the town's hard-won status. In that decade, Salem produced the first of its eight governors: LaFayette Grover and Stephen Chadwick, both Democrats.

Salem, from the 1850s onward, was actually several adjacent towns along the broad river terrace, and in 1860 Salem proper finally established a city government. The Salem of 1852, later embracing all others, went from the river to today's Cottage Street, to Mission on the south and Division on the north. North Salem and South Salem offered real competition because of their woolen and flouring mills, businesses, housing, and rough-and-ready entertainment. East Salem, on Salem's other landside, was smaller and mainly agricultural. All survived the devastating 1861 flood which ruined several competitors. By 1870 Salem annexed an eastern section, grew to over a thousand people, and by 1880 to over 2,500. Even with its suburbs, Salem, before the 1870s, remained compact as its population spread southward, then eastward.

Its people insisted on personal and civic improvement and on institutions and ways befitting a prospering town, not a crude country village. Despite a few early residents liking pistols and fist fights, the population usually remained well-behaved. Founders liked to think of it as resembling a quiet New England village—with considerably more rain. The town laid plank sidewalks, set our baseball lots, and built fences against stray animals. Its ninety-nine-foot wide streets were a source of pride. After a rash of fires in the 1860s, citizens slowly replaced wooden structures downtown with sturdy brick buildings. The wealthy built a few small mansions; the city, county, and state built public buildings of increasing size and sturdiness. By 1880 Salem was called "The City of Maples" after twenty years of tree planting on streets, in parks, and in Marion Square.

Salemites attended several small Protestant churches and the new Catholic one. They flocked to church socials, heard church bells sounding in Sunday unison, and sent missionaries abroad and among the small numbers of local Chinese and migrating native Americans. Chinese males, settled after building railroads in the 1870s, and a handful of Blacks were the only exceptions to Salem's overwhelming—then and now—white and native-born composition. The town and Catholics each began tuition-charging schools. Methodists turned the Oregon Institute for children into Willamette University and built a separate acad-

The house was moved to the Mission Mill Museum after this 1959 marker was erected. Courtesy of Statesman-Journal

Lieutenant Henry Eld, Jr., from the Wilkes Expedition in 1841, drew this picture of the Methodist Mission House, built at Mission Bottom in 1834 near the present Wheatland ferry. The Methodists moved in 1840 to what became Salem; a flood in 1861 washed away the building remains. Courtesy of Oregon State Library/WPA

emy for young pupils. Church members for years favored co-religionists as morticians and merchants. German language clubs and firms were highly visible. Salem was learning to define itself as a hard-working, moral, handsome, and education-minded town.

Bands played regularly, actors performed, and Masons and other fraternal groups organized. Literary and natural history societies and a temperance league promised civic improvement. Hunting, fishing, sailing, rowing, taking river excursions, attending dog fights, visiting the State Fair, and racing horses at the fair and after church on Sundays were popular recreations. Parades led by the active volunteer fire companies were popular, too. A gas works and water works opened. New hotels, merchant buildings and the grand Reed Opera House appeared.

Politics aroused intense loyalties; government remained minimal. The Democrats' "Salem Clique," with *The Oregon Statesman* its mouthpiece, was a power in the 1850s territory. Salem generally favored the Union and her men helped to garrison the frontier, but during the Civil War, Salem was mainly interested in her domestic pursuits, including the brief Santiam mine boom. A new telegraph brought garbled news of the distant fighting.

Salem had unpleasant aspects, too. Public hangings attracted big crowds of picnickers. Gambling, saloons, brothels, and opium dens operated. Arsonists struck downtown. Disease and early death were constants, along with flies and rubbish in streets, lots, and streams. Wells became so foul that pipes were laid to get river water, making indoor water and plumbing possible for a few. Religious, racial, and ethnic conflict was common and acceptable though not usually violent. Chinese were forced into a decrepit, downtown Chinatown.

Slow, wood-burning trains first arrived in 1870. A station was built far on the outskirts, and the line charged whatever it dared. Passenger traffic by river entered a slow decline; thereafter stagecoaches left Salem only for outlying towns and hamlets. Country roads still got short shrift since Salem deemed it cheaper to transport by rail or river. Mounting shipments of farm, forest, and manufactured products sustained the river and rail transportation which helped Salem grow, while many other landings on the Willamette slowly disappeared.

With lumber from their new sawmill, the Jason Lee, William Raymond, Lewis H. Judson, and J. L. Parrish families built the first Salem dwelling in 1841 and that fall built the Methodist Parsonage. Both are now on the grounds of the Mission Mill Museum, 260 Southeast Twelfth Street. From Joseph Gaston, Centennial History of Oregon *(Chicago, 1912)*

OREGON HISTORY
SALEM BEGAN HERE

IN THE FALL OF 1840, THE OREGON METHODIST MISSION UNDER JASON LEE DAMMED MILL CREEK BELOW THIS BRIDGE. WEST OF WHAT IS NOW LIBERTY STREET THEY ERECTED A LUMBER MILL. TWO YEARS LATER A FLOUR MILL WAS ADDED. IN 1856, THE WILLAMETTE WOOLEN MANUFACTURING COMPANY CHANNELED MORE WATER FROM THE SANTIAM RIVER TO MILL CREEK FOR A NEW FACTORY, THE FIRST POWER OPERATED WOOLEN MILLS ON THE PACIFIC COAST. THE MILLS BURNED IN 1876.

IN THE SPRING OF 1841, THE MISSIONARIES BUILT THE FIRST HOUSE IN SALEM, WHICH WITH ADDITIONS STANDS AT 960 N.E. BROADWAY. OCCUPIED BY FOUR FAMILIES INCLUDING THAT OF JASON LEE, IT LATER HOUSED SALEM'S SECOND STORE, FIRST POST OFFICE AND THE TREASURY OF THE TERRITORY OF OREGON, LATER MOVED TO THE BRICK BUILDING AT 888 N.E. LIBERTY.

CENTENNIAL MARKER
MARION COUNTY HISTORICAL SOCIETY

FIRST DWELLING HOUSE IN SALEM

Pioneer women spun yarn and wove cloth for clothing in "keeping rooms" in the rear of Salem homes. By 1895 few scenes like this remained because manufactured, inexpensive cloth and clothing had long been available. Photograph by Helen Gatch, courtesy of Oregon State Library

John D. Boon built a general store on Boon's Island in 1860 which he as Oregon Treasurer used as the State Treasury for two years. Facing Liberty Street in 1885, William Lincoln Wade's general store occupied this brick building. On its left was Harry Kelly's house and, on its right, the F. J. Babcock Furniture Store. Boon's Treasury Tavern at Broadway and High streets has occupied the old store since the 1970s. Courtesy of Statesman-Journal

Led by Salem's brass band and a We Strive and Serve sign, the first volunteer fire company, the Alert Hook and Ladder Company Number One, paraded through July 4, 1861 puddles at State and Commercial streets. The McCully and Starkey Cash Store and a log cabin, perhaps the first school moved from Marion and Commercial, are on the right. Pioneer Trust now occupies the corner. Courtesy of Salem Public Library/Maxwell

An accurate sketch of Salem in 1858 shows the first Commercial Street bridge spanning North Mill Creek and providing the village its only road access to the riches of south Marion County. The Commercial Street business area had few stores north of State Street. The wooden Courthouse of 1853, Bennett House, and the Methodist Church appeared, and, at the eastern edge, the Oregon Institute. The Salem Flouring Mill Company race and mill pond were not yet dug. Kuchel and Dresel Lithograph, courtesy of Oregon State Library

Salem investment opened the Willamette Woolen Manufacturing Company, the Pacific Coast's first woolen mill, in November 1857 near today's North Liberty and Broadway streets. It was the leading industry until an 1876 fire closed it permanently. Courtesy of Salem Public Library/Maxwell

Benjamin F. Drake and John Nation opened the Salem Iron Works in 1860 at Front and State streets. Drake and his new partner J. H. Moores rebuilt it as a two-story brick building after an 1869 fire. The well-equipped plant made iron fences for homes; also, it manufactured and repaired sawmill and farm equipment. These threshing engines were probably pictured in 1889. Some of Drake's seventeen mechanics posed about 1880. The company is now located at 2690 Northeast Blossom Drive. Workers courtesy of Statesman-Journal; building photographed by Myra E. Sperry, courtesy of Salem Public Library/Maxwell

The steamer Onward at the mouth of overflowing Pringle Creek had just rescued forty persons from the flooding Willamette. Cresting thirty-nine feet at Salem on December 31, 1861, the river nearly washed away Salem, Oregon City, and Champoeg. Courtesy of Oregon State Library

Fewer than a thousand people lived in Salem when the new 1862 bridge, probably Oregon's first covered bridge, crossed South Mill Creek from North Salem onto Commercial Street. It lasted until the 1890 flood. Probably photographed by Wiley Kentor, courtesy of Salem Public Library/Maxwell

Using water power to grind valley wheat, the Willamette Flouring Mill opened beside the Willamette Woolen Mills in 1865 where Boise Cascade now stands. Steamboats and railroads carried the flour into American and foreign commerce. Its bigger plant burned in 1899, reopening still larger in 1901. Photograph by S. E. Gray or J. H. Montgomery, courtesy of Salem Public Library/Maxwell

The crowd here is probably in front of stock barns at the first State Fair held in Salem in 1862, after its initial year near Oregon City. "Uncle" John Minto was the key to the Oregon State Agricultural Society's sponsorship of the fair, which remained basically a rough-and-ready county fair for many years. The state took responsibility for it in 1885. Courtesy of Oregon State Library

A three-sled sleighing party of Salem folk left Sol Durbin's livery and exchange stable on Commercial near State Street on January 20, 1862. Local and Oregon pursuits, including a brief Santiam mine boom, interested Salem more than the Civil War. Generally pro-Union, its troops went to garrison the frontier. Probably photographed by Wiley Kenton, courtesy of Salem Public Library/Maxwell

About 1867 the new University Hall (later Waller) dwarfed the Oregon Institute (on the left) which burned in 1872. Two more Waller Hall fires and rebuildings followed. Willamette University's claim to be the first college west of Missouri lay in its development in 1853 from Oregon Institute, an elementary school the Methodists opened in 1844 to replace the two-year-old Indian Manual Labor School in Salem. Courtesy of U. S. Bank of Oregon, Ladd and Bush Salem Branch

Curtis E. McIlwain's sedate California Bakery at 93 Court Street in 1895 began as the third house in Salem in 1843; it became the Pacific Christian Advocate *office in 1854 and after 1870 housed Sandy Burn's infamous North Star saloon. Courtesy of Salem Public Library/Maxwell*

The R. M. Wade Farm Machinery Company was a four-year-old household and farm machinery store at Commercial and Court in 1869. The store, part of Salem's boom in new businesses and construction from 1865 to 1870, remained after the company became a Portland-based, worldwide enterprise in 1893. Courtesy of Salem Public Library/Maxwell

Voluntary groups originated many American welfare institutions, including Boys and Girls Aid Society's Glen Oak Orphanage (1866-1899), pictured about 1900 when it became Salem Hospital, also established by volunteers in 1896. After 1916 the structure housed the Oregon State Hospital nurses; then it was razed. Courtesy of Oregon State Library/Trover

In 1866, Salem acquired the penitentiary from Portland, where Warden J. C. Gardner had patented the Oregon Boot (or Gardner Shackle), a shoe stirrup with attached fifteen- to twenty-five-pound weight. Used for decades to slow or punish escape-prone convicts, it broke their health and was ultimately banned. A steam-heated, gas-lit penitentiary replaced their stockade in 1871. Prisoners made items for the state and private industry and, like inmates of other state institutions, raised their own food. Pilgrim photograph by W. H. Catterlin; courtesy of U. S. Bank of Oregon, Ladd and Bush Salem Branch, boot from Oregon Historical Society

At the laying of the State Capitol cornerstone on October 8, 1873, the new Oregon Home for the Sick was the white building in upper background. This private hospital did not last long, since the ill preferred home visits from doctors as well as whiskey, home remedies, and quack medicines. Photograph by Joseph Buchtel, courtesy of Salem Public Library/Maxwell

The Reed Opera House, completed 1869-1870, held ground floor shops, a saloon, a hotel, the State Library, and the Supreme Court. When pictured about 1880, its upstairs auditorium had twenty years left as Salem's most prestigious center for social, cultural, and political events. Later devoted to mercantile businesses, it is now part of the Reed Opera House Mall. Courtesy of Salem Public Library/Maxwell

For almost a hundred years, many of Oregon's and Salem's most important political, economic, and cultural decisions occurred—unofficially, but very definitely—in a single hotel at Commercial and Ferry streets. Pictured between 1870 and 1889 as the Chemeketa House, it became the Willamette Hotel (1890-1909) and then the Marion Hotel; it later became then the Marion Hotel, later the Marion Motor Hotel (1910-1971). Courtesy of Salem Public Library/Maxwell

After 1874 "The White Corner" was Salem's mercantile center for the Breyman Brothers and, when pictured after 1901, for Holverson and Yantis' men's store at Court and Commercial streets. Modernized, the structure still exists. Courtesy of Salem Public Library/Maxwell

Ladd and Bush Bank established an imposing, ornate, cast-iron presence on State and Commercial streets in 1869. By 1871 gas street lamps had replaced the flickering oil lamps. By 1880 wooden sidewalks kept pedestrians out of abundant dust and mud in front of the enlarged bank. Shade trees were planted soon after this picture was taken. Courtesy of Salem Public Library/Maxwell

Viewed across a barren Willson Park in 1870 were Court Street homes of John H. Albert (corner) and to the left, of George Holman, and (with cupola) of Joseph Holman, father of George and father-in-law of John Albert. St. Joseph Church, dating from 1863, and in 1871 serving 150 Catholics, was behind the Albert House. From Oregon Historical Society

Points of interest in 1876 Salem included the Capitol; the three-year-old Courthouse; flour mills in South Salem; a ferry landing at State Street and a steam boat dock at Trade Street; the railroad; a wooden water tower on Water Street; and Willson Park, extending from the Capitol to the Courthouse. The Agricultural Building, just east of the covered bridge on Trade Street, made items from farm machinery to furniture. The artist added a rear portion to the Courthouse and a dome to the Capitol and was also inaccurate about the Agricultural Building. From Bird's Eye View of Salem in 1876; drawn by E. S. Glover from a photo by F. A. Smith, courtesy of Oregon State Library

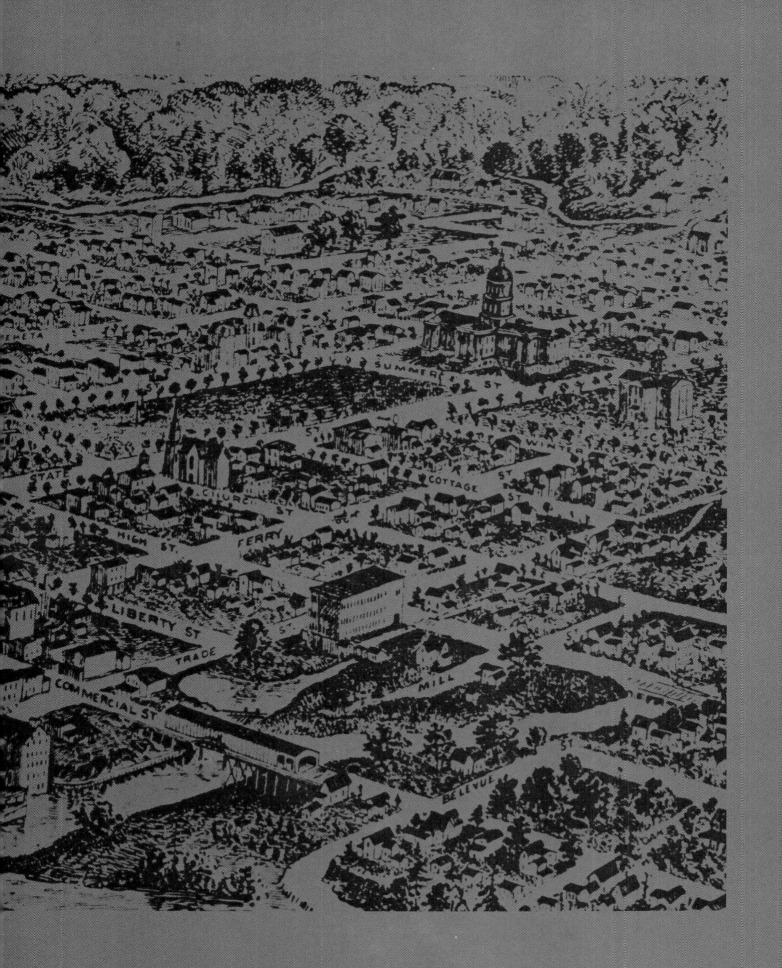

Chapter Two

1880–1900

About 1894 Willson Park had shaped trees and a quarter-mile bicycle track at its lower end. Looking westward along Court Street from the Capitol dome, the city hall was under construction, but no post office had appeared. Photograph by F. H. Welch, courtesy of Oregon State Library/Trover

Music, particularly when displaying a young person's accomplishments, brought pleasure to many Victorian parlors. Here, about 1897, Minnie Breyman was accompanied in the home of her parents, Mr. and Mrs. Eugene Breyman, at Court and Church streets. Courtesy of Mr. and Mrs. Evan Boise

A small, proud town emerged from the wooden cottages and mills beside the Willamette. Between 1880 and 1900 Salem grew from some 2,500 to more than 4,000 persons. Most of its founders had passed from the scene. They were replaced by migrants, largely native-born except for numerous Germans and Chinese, and by those born into Salem's big families.

"Salem does not aspire to become a great commercial center" but rather an agricultural distribution town and a "center of arts and manufacturers," the Board of Trade proclaimed in 1893. It had never been nor wished to be a boom town, it added. Pre-eminence in Oregon was recognizably Portland's. Salem preferred to stress its status as a capital. It encouraged expansion of state schools for the blind and deaf and the penitentiary and obtained a new Indian School in nearby Chemewa, an Insane Asylum, and a reformatory. Local leaders bargained and struck deals at the Willamette Hotel and celebrated at the gubernatorial inauguration of hometowner William Lord.

What Salem sought most was leadership in the mid-Willamette Valley. It wished to draw into its economic and social order the farms and hamlets reached easily by train or sternwheeler and, strenuously, by rough roads. Townsfolk wanted the wheat most valley farmers raised, their hops, wool, and fruit from the orchards first planted in the 1880s and 1890s. Salem would process the crops and also make or sell supplies its visitors and residents needed; thus, it would furnish the services and amenities of a "town."

In Salem you could have teeth pulled, a deed drawn and, by 1896, care in a hospital. You could join a church with a big new building, any of several active fraternal lodges, numerous clubs or the new sports-minded YMCA. You could enroll in public school, at Sacred Heart Academy, at the short-lived Friends Polytechnic Institute, or in the influential Willamette University. After 1886 you could cross into Salem proper from Polk County by

bridge, not the old ferry. Strollers could admire the majestic Cascades, a green park and square, the public buildings, and the brick commercial and factory structures named for their owners. You could find housing or shop space on the newly extended State, High, and Court streets. Job hunters could find long hours in local mills, stores, shops, and farms; seasonal labor in nearby fields and orchards.

Most of the year Salem also choked on blowing dust or mired in the mud in the streets and country roads. Eastern and southern Oregon families knew it was best to start with wagons and exhibition stock a week prior to the State Fair. By the 1890s, however, some worked in Salem on behalf of street paving, removal of hitching racks from main streets, and laying of concrete walks and cross walks. Meanwhile, people endured uneven or broken plank sidewalks with their underside of rotting matter and noxious smells. And they probably felt safer because of a paid fire department after 1893. Its new steam pumpers, housed in a city hall built in 1897, had improved city water pressure and lines. Still, many missed the colorful, club-like volunteer fire fighting companies.

By 1890, you could ride a trolley and sometimes drink water drawn from a faucet or turn on a gas or electric light in Salem. A few street lamps had appeared where businesses clustered. Nothing had yet been done about trash in alleys or streams. You could talk on the telephone to a few places, send a telegram anywhere, and read local newspapers and farm journals. You could hear or play music, attend a lecture, observe or participate in a parade—lots of them—and spend a glorious week at the fair. You could play or watch many sports, hunt at the edge of town, and fish Salem's streams, ditches, and river. A few minutes from the business section, you could test who had the fastest horse. An easy walk brought you to saloons, gambling, and opium dens and bordellos. Only with real effort could you remain anonymous in Salem by the turn-of-the-century.

By 1900, many of the old pioneering ways had disappeared. Salemites no longer freely attended weddings and funerals without invitations. Groups charged membership fees. Ornate mansions now clustered on certain streets and dotted others in a Salem where most people still lived in wooden cottages with barns and outbuildings. Fences had come down or were devoted more for show than for fending off animals. Where streetcars ran, neighborhoods developed at greater distances from downtown.

Salem was healthy enough to recover fully from the terrible flood of February 1890. However, it endured real hardship during the severe national depression of 1893-1897, which bankrupted a bank, the State Insurance Company, the trolley line, and other firms. In 1897, the Klondike Gold Rush was much welcomed since it fueled a demand for Salem products and offered some residents an opportunity to seek riches in mining. Also, men hurried to volunteer for the Spanish-American War in 1898. The town managed to enter the new century with much of its old optimism intact.

In 1885 the Oregon and California Railroad (later Southern Pacific) replaced its burned depot on the original site, which was now closer to an expanded downtown. The horse-drawn streetcars were used only in 1889. Drivers worked in three-hour shifts from 6 am to 9 pm for two dollars a day. The owner, Dr. Henry J. Minthorn, also had a real estate office and a young nephew—the future president Herbert Hoover—living with him and working in the office. Courtesy of Statesman-Journal

A locomotive headed eastward toward the present Twelfth Street along the Trade Street branch connecting riverfront industries to the Southern Pacific main line in 1889. The piled wood was used not only at the Churchill Sash and Door Manufacturing Company but also at the Western Fanning Mill, which made devices for processing grain. Courtesy of Salem Public Library/Maxwell

From early tintypes to modern color photography, Salem has enjoyed pictures of its children. Children loved the goat, donkey, pony, and dog carts the wealthy parents and photographers owned. Captain Jim Smith's son was in a donkey cart at Court and Commercial streets about 1885. Courtesy of Mr. and Mrs. Evan Boise

Willamette Valley wheat and Salem flour were basic sternwheeler cargo during the 1890s. The Capitol Mills, erected in 1877, is on the left. Williamette Valley Flouring Mills (Scotch Mills), on the right, opened in 1882 and burned in 1904. Courtesy of Salem Public Library/Maxwell

About 1888 the William M. Hoag carried excursionists serenaded by a band under the "Big Bridge," Salem's (and Oregon's) first vehicle span across the Willamette, opened in December of 1886. By the turn of the century, Salem steamboats carried more passengers than freight, which now moved mainly by rail. Courtesy of Al Jones

The Holman ferry crossed toward the Eola Hills before the 1886 opening of Salem's first bridge over the Willamette. Salem ferries to Polk County had operated since the 1840s. Courtesy of Al Jones

Steamboats at the foot of Trade Street during the bad February 1890 flood. Ramona of the Graham fleet carried passengers and cargo. Gypsy was one of the smallest shallow draft craft on the Willamette River; Ruth was one of the fastest. Courtesy of Oregon State Library

Sun Lung outside his laundry at 105 Court Street, adjoining Staiger Marble Works, probably in 1889. The oak tree, alone remained of a picnic ground grove where Colonel Edward Dickenson Baker's rousing July 4, 1860, speech helped catapult Baker into the United States Senate. A Union Army volunteer, he soon died in battle. Courtesy of Salem Public Library/Maxwell

Children of a Chinese servant about 1897 when some 300 Chinese lived in high-rent, unhealthy wooden hovels which also housed their restaurants and laundries, in a Chinatown around Liberty and State streets. Anti-Chinese feeling prevailed in Salem, but there were apparently no physical attacks. Courtesy of Mr. and Mrs. Evan Boise

First appearing in the 1850s, bands supplemented popular homemade music and fiddle contests. The Salem Amusement Company band, led by an ex-circus musician, was Salem's finest during the 1880s. Rear, left to right, were: Joe Farrar, Rube Glaze, John Farrar, Fred Levy, John Coomer, M. L. Meyers, George Mack, Mack Long, and Eugene England. Front, left to right, were: Ed Crawford, William McElroy, Frank Hars, Ted Piper, Dick Riley, Theodore Potter, Ed Long, and John Chase. Courtesy of Salem Public Library/Maxwell

City of Salem, all gingerbread and green shutters, offered famous river excursions from 1875 to 1895. The Masonic Band serenaded families at the Trade Street dock one day in 1885 before Captain Raabe managed to run the sternwheeler onto a sandbar near Albany. Salemites enjoyed Sunday excursions to Albany or Corvallis and, perhaps, then on by train to the coast at Newport. From Oregon Historical Society/Cronise

A turn-of-the-century classroom of the important Sacred Heart Academy, operated by the Sisters of the Holy Name of Jesus since 1863. Located on "Piety Hill" near St. John Church after 1873, the Academy—during a thirty-year co-educational period—moved again in 1932; finally, in 1956, again exclusively for females, it moved to 3750 Northeast Lancaster Drive. Courtesy of Oregon State Library/Trover

One late nineteenth century melodrama at the Reed Opera House involved a rescue at sea. Traveling shows during state fairs and legislative sessions came to the Reed and after 1900 to the Grand Opera Theater in the new Odd Fellows Building. Theater folk considered Salem a poor theater town. Courtesy of Oregon State Library/Trover

A bearded "Mode" Harbord and Perry O. Mauzey, posed with a loyal companion, were all the police a generally well-behaved Salem needed in the 1880s. Courtesy of Salem Public Library/Maxwell

Well into the 1910s, Salem seldom worried about flies, rats, cats or health when displaying food in stores and on sidewalks. McCrow and Willard Meat Market in 1891, at either its 205 or 316 Commercial Street location, competed with other butcher shops in ample displays, duly recorded by commercial photographers. From Oregon Historical Society/Cronise

Hay wagons stand outside T. B. Wait Hardware and Farm Machinery store at State and Commercial streets about 1885. Area farmers, their main crops wheat and hops before 1900, crowded Salem streets with their wagons and carriages on Saturdays and holidays. From Oregon Historical Society/Cronise

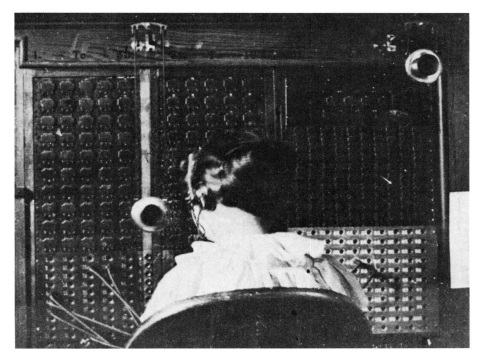

The Oregon Telephone and Telegraph Company had its switchboard in Smith and Steiner's drugstore, 241 Commercial Street, from 1890 to 1906. Local service for a dozen subscribers began in 1884 through the Western Union office. By 1898, 115 Salem customers could connect to Oregon and California cities; by 1914, customers called across the continent. Courtesy of Oregon State Library

Salem between 1851 and 1972 had thirty-one newspapers, few lasting more than a year or two. Will H. Parry's first Capital Journal *on March 1, 1888, faced an entrenched* The Oregon Statesman. *Produced on a hand-lever press, the new Republican paper devoted almost half of its four pages to advertisements. It later supported the Democratic Party. Courtesy of* Statesman-Journal

The annual stallion shows, all-male affairs, occurred each spring beginning in 1880 to provide for horse buying, trading, and services. This one, early in the 1880s, centered around the typically muddy State and Commercial streets. Photograph by William P. Johnson, from Oregon Historical Society/Cronise

Everything about horses before the automotive age interested Salem. Here, at the turn of the century, Robert Adams from Polk County widely exhibited Oregon Beauty for its unusual nine-foot mane and thirteen-foot tail. Courtesy of Oregon State Library/Trover

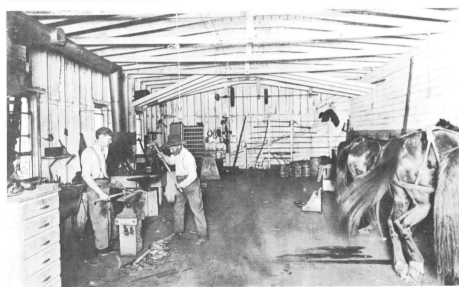

Work proceeded at A. C Schafer's Blacksmith Shop at Mill and Commercial streets late in the nineteenth century. Courtesy of Salem Public Library/Maxwell

Along North Commercial Street during the 1880s, Scriber and Pohle Blacksmith Shop, sign painters, and other craftspeople plied their trades. Here, Herman Pohle holds the wheel. Until their decline in the 1920s, blacksmith shops and livery stables, replete with chewing tobacco and horse liniment ads and spitoons, were important male gathering-places offering escape from Salem's more genteel establishments. Courtesy of Salem Public Library/Maxwell

In 1885 small farms with outbuildings dotted a sparsely settled East Salem. The photographer, on the East Salem School roof, looked eastward along Marion Street. Women played baseball in the school yard, now the site of a Safeway store on Center Street. Photograph by William P. Johnson, from Oregon Historical Society/Cronise

Salem's Alert (left) and Capital (right) companies in front of the teams from Eugene, Astoria, Lebanon and elsewhere were photographed on North Commercial Street on September 9, 1886, at the Annual (since 1882) Firemen's Association of Oregon Tourney. The Capital was known as the Dude Company because of its "society" membership. Photograph by William P. Johnson, from Oregon Historical Society/Cronise

One of Salem's four volunteer companies, probably Hose Company No. 3, prepared for the wet hose cart race on North Commercial Street in 1886. The physical expansion of Salem, plus gradual introduction of horse-drawn steam pumpers, doomed the large companies that were needed to pull and operate equipment. The year 1893 brought a professional department to Salem. Photograph by William P. Johnson, from Oregon Historical Society/Cronise

The state militia in Civil War-like uniforms on North Commercial at Court Street attracted casual watchers, September 10, 1883. Photograph by Sperry Johnson, courtesy of Salem Public Library/Maxwell

About 1888 the post office staff in front of the Smith Building at Ferry and Commercial streets, now a parking lot, included, left to right: George Hatch, Ben Taylor (on bicycle), Captain Lyman S. Scott (postmaster), Zadie Palmer, Dick and Ella Dearborn, Glen Turner, and Scott Bozarth. Courtesy of Salem Public Library/Maxwell

Its marshal, E. C. Cross on horseback and Miss Columbia in a carriage led the July 4, 1892, parade at Court and Commercial streets. In 1889 seventeen Italianate brick stores had replaced pioneer wooden ones on Commercial streets. In 1889, seventeen Italianate brick stores had peaked in sunrise to late-night activities during the 1890s. Courtesy of Salem Public Library/Maxwell

A Mr. Taylor, John McNary, George Collins, and Jasper Minto in front of Fashion Stables (now the Odd Fellows Temple) at Court and High streets, after a successful hunting trip in 1889. Plentiful small birds and game were only a quick walk to the town's edge until the 1920s. Photograph by Myra E. Sperry, from Oregon Historical Society/Cronise

Skaters had fun on the South Salem Slough near the Salem Flouring Mill (in the background) about January 1899. Mild winters rarely permitted skating here. Courtesy of Frank Cross

Oregonians had recently joined the new national craze for bicycling when these professional bike racers rested between heats at the Oregon State Fair in 1896. A tax on bicycles supported Salem bicycle paths leading into the countryside. From Oregon Historical Society

In the 1890s a bartender posed probably at the fancy Talkington and Aiken Saloon in the Reed Opera House. It was a meeting place for businessmen and farmers, while other saloons served as informal social clubs for workingmen. From Oregon Historical Society/Cronise

In the 1890s Joseph G. Fontaine's Saloon and Billiard Hall, 311 State Street, was a popular outlet for Salem's flourishing breweries, first begun in the 1860s. Courtesy of Salem Public Library/Maxwell

The flood damage in February 1890 was of major proportions in Salem, worse than that in January 1881 but not as bad as the flood of December 1861. Looking northward down High Street, Pringle Creek backwater (five days before the river crested) had already destroyed the High Street bridge and flooded homes and businesses. The flooded river also destroyed homes and strewed piled lumber at the foot of Chemeketa Street. Photographs by Myra E. Sperry, from Oregon Historical Society/Cronise

The Reverend and Mrs. Daniel Staver of Forest Grove and Marietta Gilbert of Salem stood in the doorway of the First Congregational Church, Liberty and Center streets, during the state-wide Congregational Association meeting in 1890. Salem's many churches and church organizations had certainty and influence. Church members also favored businesses owned by co-religionists. From Oregon Historical Society

Willamette University and Salem have always profoundly affected one another. Before 1900, the university never enrolled more than 100 strictly chaperoned students, drawn mainly from locally prominent families. Here students demonstrated the serious interests expected of them late in the nineteenth century. Most suppressed smiles. From Oregon Historical Society/Cronise

Students Burt Savage, Billy Babcock, and Mark Savage (left to right) played on the joint Willamette-YMCA football team in 1892. Separate teams came in 1894. Courtesy of Willamette University

The university suffered a serious blow when Waller Hall, its major building, burned on September 16, 1891, in the first of three fires and rebuildings. Courtesy of Oregon State Library

The pumping plant of the Salem Water Company, featured on an 1895 postcard, brought water from the Willamette to increasing numbers of customers. The few sewers, introduced late in the 1880s, also emptied into the same river and into North Mill Creek. Before World War I, the creek, river, and downtown alleys were routine dumping grounds. Courtesy of Salem Public Library/Maxwell

The Marion County Fruit Palace at the State Fair, September 14 1891, was covered by over 100 varieties of fruit then in season in the county. Branches on it were eight or more feet long. Since the 1880s, fruit in immense variety had begun to replace grain as the major area crop—and began to redirect Salem's agricultural interests. Courtesy of U. S. Bank of Oregon, Ladd and Bush Salem Branch

Fire in 1895 destroyed the Thomas Kay Woolen Mill which Kay, son-in-law Charles P. Bishop, and others established in 1889 after a fourteen-year lapse in Salem woolen manufacturing. Rebuilt in 1896 after the company and townsfolk quickly pledged capital, it prospered immediately from the Alaska Gold Rush and the Spanish-American War. It now forms the core of the Mission Mill Museum. Courtesy of Carlisle B. Roberts

A streetcar, about 1892, rounds the curve in front of the A. N. Gilbert home, Liberty and Chemeketa streets, on the way to the Insane Asylum (later Oregon State Hospital). After 1890 twelve miles of electric trolley lines, plus extention of city water and electric services, brought growth outside the compact core, and Salem's first suburbanization began. Courtesy of Salem Public Library/ Maxwell

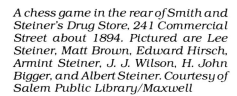

A chess game in the rear of Smith and Steiner's Drug Store, 241 Commercial Street about 1894. Pictured are Lee Steiner, Matt Brown, Edward Hirsch, Armint Steiner, J. J. Wilson, H. John Bigger, and Albert Steiner. Courtesy of Salem Public Library/Maxwell

Heavily Republican post-Civil War Salem took politics seriously. Certain families, however, remained adamantly Democratic. When merchant George Meyers (left) and dentist George Wright (right) lost an election bet on November 24, 1884, the crowd watching them saw cordwood in front of the Dugan Brothers plumbing shop at 260 Commercial Street included Dr. W. J. Meredith (wearing a plug hat), George Boynter (leaning against a post), and Philo Armstrong in blacksmith's apron. Courtesy of Salem Public Library/Maxwell

Working people often lived in boarding houses and ate in small restaurants. These men, probably at The Spa at 114 State Street around the turn of the century, kept their hats on. Gas, manufactured from coal, lit the counter. Photograph by Tom Cronise, courtesy of U. S. Bank of Oregon, Ladd and Bush Salem Branch

A Salem hotel lobby, probably late in the 1880s, displayed a modern Singer Sewing Machine. By then, hotels were available for all price ranges and tastes and, like boarding houses, overflowed when the legislature met. Courtesy of Ed Culp

Here, John Gulliver West drove the carriage while his daughter, Nean West, sat sidesaddle; his son Fred West, held a horse, and his grandson, Walter West, sat on the steps of the West home, Oak and University streets in 1895. Oswald West, John's son and a future governor, was not present. Pouter pigeons roosted over the barn, which with other outbuildings, pastures, trees, fences, and windmills gave Salem a semi-rural look well into this century. Courtesy of Oregon State Library/Trover

Warmed by a kerosene heater, a young gentleman reads in his bedroom decorated with many carefully arrayed photographs around the turn of the century. In nineteenth century Salem the wealthy enjoyed photographing their own lives. They, and the few commercial photographers, alone had cameras. Courtesy of Oregon State Library/Trover

When Anna Strong (front right, skirt out) had a party, older guests on the rear row included, Professor Little (far left) and, left to right: Leona Hirsch (in hat), Jessie Breyman, Chester Murphy, Gerty Hirsch, Joe Baumgartner, unidentified, future Senator Charles McNary, unidentified, and future Governor Ben Olcott. Courtesy of Oregon State Library/Trover

The A. N. Gilbert family camped with their flag at Slab Creek in 1880. This and other prominent families summered at the ocean and in mountains, woods, and rustic inns near Salem during the 1880s and 1890s. Fathers returned weekdays to conduct Salem businesses and professions. Courtesy of Oregon State Library

Vacationing near Seal Rock in 1894 were "The Bear Creek Party" including Judge George H. Bingham (pole), William Bingham (behind him), Judge George H. Burnett (boots, standing far left), Werner Breyman (seated behind him), Clifford Brown (boy below Judge Bingham) and William Brown (white helmet). Photograph by Myra E. Sperry, courtesy of Mr. and Mrs. Evan Boise

The Reuben Boise family and friends lived comfortably at Mehama in 1890. Camping for prominent families meant extra tents to house dining and living rooms and servants. Courtesy of Mr. and Mrs. Evan Boise

Louis Kibele (left) and Walt Delaney (right) before 1893 worked in front of dangerous open belts and exposed wires of Salem's first electric power plant installed by Thomas Holman in 1886 at High and Trade streets. Most homes still lit by kerosene lamps and cooked and heated by wood into the new century. Courtesy of Oregon State Library/Trover

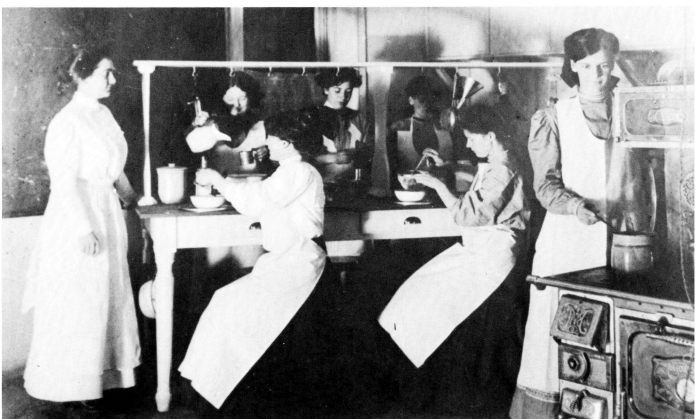

A home economics class at the School for Deaf Mutes about 1898. Oregon was unusual in that a deaf man, William Stephens Smith, had founded the school (as the Deaf and Dumb School in 1870), and the state has always educated deaf children separately from blind children. Courtesy of Oregon State School for the Deaf

About 1896 the Salem Labor Exchange Association met, held social gatherings, and stored goods for barter in a North River Road barn near Pine Street. Members of the national group tried to replace money with bartering during the terrible depression of 1893-1897 which, in Salem, bankrupted numerous businesses. Courtesy of Salem Public Library/Maxwell

Pictured in 1889, the Capitol had a year earlier added columned porticoes at front and rear. It still kept the fence against stray animals but had not yet added the dome. Courtesy of Oregon State Library

J. D. Irvine, doorkeeper, looked at the camera (right, front) when the Senate was photographed in 1895. A facetious local saying was that Salem's best crops were the state legislature and State Fair. Courtesy of Oregon State Library/Trover

Chapter Three

1900–1920

The Third Regiment of the Oregon National Guard marched from High onto State Street as bicycle riders kept pace during the July 4, 1900, parade. Not having seen action during the Spanish-American War, troops drawn from the regiment were fighting Filipino nationalists in 1900. Courtesy of U.S. Bank of Oregon, Ladd and Bush Salem Branch

Participants in the Cherry Fair parade unselfconsciously displayed patriotism in a manner common in American celebrations in 1908. They were parked at Front and Hickory streets. The Cherry Fair eventually supplanted Independence Day as Salem's major event. Photograph by George M. Weister, courtesy of Willamette University

"Adam and Eve Lost Paradise. We Have Found It." This slogan, announced by the Greater Salem Commercial Club in 1902, was a vision widely shared locally. Most thought the town was paradise-like in its bountiful land, in its natural beauty, and in the pleasant lives and attractive community built by its people.

Certainly the Salem area was garden-like in its flourishing orchards, which in these decades replaced many wheat farms. Huge amounts of fruit as well as abundant flax, nuts, hops, and wool came into the appreciative town. Salem itself seemed heavenly to anyone liking to fish or canoe in its streams and river, casually hunt just outside its boundaries, or vacation in nearby woods, mountains, and beaches. The town was also delightfully uncluttered. Trees shaded the streets; roses blossomed around Willson Park. On the outskirts, fenced home lots were bounded by family pastures or small farms. After 1907 concrete sidewalks and paved streets began lifting Salem from its old dust and mud-spattered existence.

Also, Salem, considered itself as a special preserve of personal industry, sober earnestness, self control, and moral integrity in a nation seemingly marked by pell-mell city and industrial ways, social discord, and, to Salemites, unduly questioned values. Family, morality and tradition were important and remained so in Salem. Its numerous churches, lodges, clubs, and businesses, aided by the schools and newspapers, helped wrap Salem, like other Oregon towns and cities, in its own world of its residents' activities.

Challenge to Salem's ways and viewpoints, represented by the craft unionists, the occasional socialist, the radical Industrial Workers of the World organizer in 1912, were minor. Racial and ethnic minorities, Chinese and Japanese especially, kept low profiles, lending color and vitality to a Salem whose values they often shared. But certainly not everyone agreed about everything. There were two hard-fought elections before Salem voted dry in 1913. Nearby hamlets then received drinkers from Salem; farmers along the way made profits from pulling their cars from ditches. Gambling and opium dens still operated. Prostitution continued in boarding houses and hotels after official closing of the notorious "Peppermint

Flat."

Salem also prided itself on its modernity and progressive outlook, exhibited by its comfortable growth, new technology, and urban amenities. Between 1900 and 1910 the population more than tripled to 14,094, largely because of a 1903 annexation of North, South, and East Salem. In 1910, Salem took in land to the west, in 1920, the state fairgrounds. Homes filled city lots and straggled toward the expanding city limits. Hopeful investors laid out additions reachable by trolley or car. A small housing boom began at the end of the First World War.

Downtown began to appear more like a small city than a farm trading and service center. Small boat yards launched wooden ships into the Willamette River. Businesses shifted in the new century from Commercial Street to a concentrated mercantile zone around Liberty and State streets. Between 1900 and 1913 new Odd Fellows and Masonic buildings, an armory for the National Guard and civic events, and a Supreme Court building were erected. The shabby Willamette Hotel became a remodeled, enlarged Marion Hotel. Street lighting, traffic lights, and alley cleanups accompanied new concrete sidewalks and street paving downtown. Salem now acquired Waite Fountain to grace Willson Park and its first public statue. After 1900 the Grand Opera Theater in the new Odd Fellow's Hall replaced Reed's Opera House as the town showcase.

The wealthy and adventurous bought the first noisy gasoline, steam, and electric cars. Businesses began replacing horses with trucks, and a taxi company opened. Salemites had their first car thefts and accidents and learned to avoid their customary strolls in the street. Sally Bush's first and last venture at the wheel—straight into a drug store—became part of Miss Sally's legend.

The automobile began loosening the old hold of the railroad and steamship lines on mid-Willamette Valley passengers and freight. Confident business interests successfully lobbied for better farm-to-Salem market roads, city street paving, and the improvement of roads to Portland and other Oregon cities. The Oregon Electric Interurban line came to Salem in 1905 and, in the next few years, offered convenient daily travel to many places between Portland and Eugene. Tiny West Salem secured a rail stop, then a railroad bridge into Salem. Salem received a new train station and in 1918 replaced its dangerous Willamette River bridge with one meant to handle automobiles and trucks.

In 1907 Salem enhanced its importance as the capital city by securing a constitutional requirement that all state institutions locate in Marion County unless excluded by state vote. The Hillcrest School of Oregon for disturbed females and a state Tuberculosis Hospital opened. Mental retardates were transferred from the Insane Asylum in 1908 to what became the Fairview Training Center. Other state institutions were encouraged to expand. The state's only flax mill was installed at the penitentiary to benefit Oregon flax growers. Again, the town furnished governors: Oswald West in

Looking eastward in 1902 from the Capitol dome with Court Street angling right from the foreground. Salem had both electrical lines and lots still used to graze family cows and horses. The Insane Asylum tower was in the distance. Courtesy of Oregon State Library

1911 and Ben Olcott in 1919.

In the new century, Salem made fruit processing its leading industry. Farm co-ops and private concerns started or enlarged small canneries and dehydration and pressing plants. It became acceptable for women and children, not just men, to work seasonally in canneries, hop fields, and orchards. To encourage better cherries, the Elks in 1903 began a small annual Cherry Festival. As official Cherry City of the World, Salem expanded the festival in 1908 into an all-encompassing exhibition and celebration of orchardists and itself. The Cherrians first appeared in 1913 to march twice yearly, to boost the town, and to arrange a Blossom Day to draw visitors by car to blossoming orchards near Salem. "Trail 'Em to Salem" was the 1913 watchword for the growth-minded. The *Oregon Statesman* predicted 50,000 would soon live in the city. Only 17,679 made it by 1920.

Thus, past and present continued its habitual co-existence during Salem's first two decades. Fewer pioneers gathered at State Fair reunions, but Civil War veterans still honored parades. A few poorer folk still arrived in Salem by covered wagons. Barns and sheds housed cars, yet a few livery stables lingered into the 1920s. Sedate band concerts drew attendance at Marion Square, but many went to the new nickelodeons, the first silent film theaters. The first wireless message left Salem in 1909. After 2,000 paid to see the fair's initial auto race fizzle in 1910, horse racing retained its popularity. Salem would have preferred that two local tinkerers, Schovell and Taylor, had been the first locally to fly a plane but still applauded the showman Eugene Ely, who beat them to it. Even after Salem men marched away to war in 1917—to return largely unhurt in 1918 in the same cloud of patriotism—the town tried to continue its tested ways.

Salem Indian Training School floats passed down North Commercial Street during the July 4, 1902, parade. Two wigwams, an Uncle Sam and four war-painted native Americans from Chemawa, rode the first float; the second was devoted to the school's Industrial Arts training. Courtesy of Salem Public Library/ Maxwell

Wrecking of the northbound California express near the Salem depot on December 7, 1901, killed the cab crew. Salem long remembered steamboat explosions and rail wrecks. The U. S. in the 1900s had the industrial world's worst train accident record. Courtesy of Salem Public Library/Maxwell

In 1912 passengers at the Southern Pacific depot in Salem could ride the McKeon gasoline coach twenty-seven miles to Black Rock—or leave for anywhere in the country. From 1905 to 1933 Oregon Electric Interurban Line trains also served Salem daily. After 1908, Interurban trains went down High Street to their new Oregon Building depot. Courtesy of Oregon State Library

Dedication of the Salem-Falls City and Western Railroad bridge across to Salem on March 15, 1913, and their own depot encouraged tiny West Salem to incorporate in 1914. Trains which first arrived in West Salem in 1909 had crossed the Willamette by ferry. *Courtesy of Salem Public Library/Maxwell*

Wagon drivers proceeded slowly, about 1908, knowing the 1891 Willamette River bridge was unsafe. It replaced the one destroyed by flood in 1890 and was torn down after the Center Street bridge opened in 1918. *Photograph by George M. Weister, from Oregon Historical Society*

Prince and Veda Byrd strolled after the dedication of the Center Street bridge in a flurry of World War I patriotism on August 2, 1918. Designing the bridge to handle cars and trucks recognized the new transportation era but not the explosive growth in traffic which followed. *Courtesy of Frank Cross*

Members of the Portland Auto Club at the new Bligh Theater on State Street in 1912 knew that to brave Oregon's rutted dirt roads—few did from November to April—they better be rigged for towing. Otto Wilson in 1903 had introduced the first of the gas, battery and steam cars noisily operating over Salem streets. George Leslie had exhibited a steam cylinder vehicle in 1874. Courtesy of Oregon State Library/Trover

Distrustful of newly paved streets, some Salem car owners brought chains on November 30, 1910, to the Oregon Development League meeting. They gathered in front of the once-shabby Willamette Hotel. In 1910, it had lost its chimneys, changed its roof, and emerged as a grander Marion Hotel. Photograph by Tom Cronise, courtesy of Oregon State Library

The Salem fire department proudly exhibited its steam pumpers on Court Street about 1906. People visited fire stations to pet and feed the horses, and they were thrilled when horses dashed with fire equipment through the streets. Courtesy of Salem Public Library/Maxwell

The Yew Park suburban district temporarily revived volunteer firemen in the late 1890s. The Yew Park Hose Team at Thirteenth and Leslie streets used an antiquated hand pumper long-retired by Salem. In 1901 the Hose Team became part of the Salem Fire Department. Courtesy of Oregon State Library/Trover

The shallow draft sternwheeler Julius landed at the Spaulding Logging Company, South Front and Ferry streets, about 1908. The mill furnished mainly block and slab wood and later added sash and door manufacturing. Railroads, not the two steamship lines serving Salem, carried most of the town's fast freight in this era. Courtesy of Al Jones

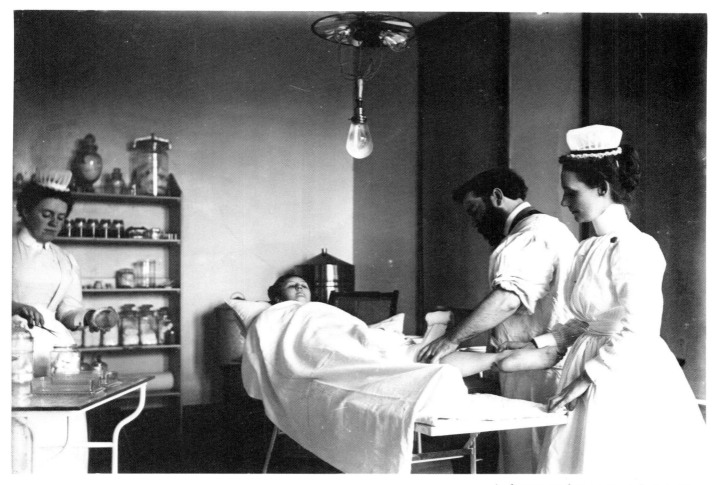

A doctor and nurses at Salem Hospital, later renamed Salem General Hospital in 1926, treated a patient early in the century. The Mennonite Church in December 1916 opened a second one, twelve-bed Deaconess Hospital, renamed Salem Memorial Hospital in 1947 when the church connection ended. Courtesy of Oregon State Library/Trover

The Capital Lumbering Company, at the foot of Ferry Street, was the principal sawmill in the Salem vicinity from 1866 to 1914. The office, plant, and workmen in its yard were photographed in 1901. Courtesy of Oregon State Library/Trover

Fletch Long and Roma Hunter (at far left) stand with owner Curtis B. Cross (in a suit) at the E. C. Cross and Son Market, 354 State Street, about 1910. Butcher shops routinely displayed offerings indoors and outside. Cross and others wove paper through hanging meat each Christmas season. Courtesy of Frank Cross

Ditch diggers lay pipe, probably in the Highland district, in the 1910s. The extension of water and sewer lines meant improved health, safety, and convenience for Salem and also encouraged housing in such new outlying areas. Photograph by Richard Lowenfeld, courtesy of Salem Public Works Department

Salem Flouring Mills reopened in 1901 after a devastating 1899 fire. With a rebuilt mill still using water-power, it soon produced more than 400,000 bushels of flour annually for American and foreign sale. Probably photographed by Dr. S. A. Davis Bean, courtesy of Boise Cascade Paper Group, Salem, Oregon

The D. S Bentley and Company ran a building supply and transfer company at 319 Front Street in 1902. Courtesy of Oregon State Library/Trover

Ethelbert C. Case travelled for Dr. Baker's Medicines, Extracts and Spices in Salem and its countryside during the 1910s. Both humans and animals received the supposed benefits. Courtesy of Oregon State Library/Trover

Puss and Tab, favorite horses in Salem parades, pulled the ornate W. T. Rigdon hearse from 142 Court Street about 1900. Winfield T. Rigdon became a mortician in 1892, and the firm operates today as Rigdon-Ransom Colonial Funeral Chapel at 299 Northeast Cottage Street. Courtesy of Ed Culp

The owner of the household goods, as was customary, accompanied the new Kapphahn Transfer Company truck and crew about 1910. Ernest L. Kapphahn, at the wheel, began his firm with horses in 1909. The family was agent for the electric interurban railroad and also ran a candy store and restaurant in the Oregon Building. Courtesy of Ernest L. Kapphahn

Hamman Stage Lines in 1913 carried freight and up to twelve passengers on its Salem, Stayton, Mill City run. It issued lap robes in bad weather. Begun in 1909 in a livery stable, today it is a regular and charter service at 2555 Southeast Twenty-Fifth Street. Courtesy of Hamman Stage Lines

This picture of E. T. Barnes' New York Racket Store at 318 Commercial Street dramatized its Brown's Shoe stock about 1905. Salem was in a buying mood in this prosperous era. Courtesy of Salem Public Library/Maxwell

Farmer and later Kay Woolen Mills cashier Roy V. Ohmart had one of Salem's thirty-three groceries in 1909. This one had a suburban site on Liberty Road across from the Odd Fellows Cemetery. Grocery home deliveries by wagon and later by truck were common well into the 1940s. Courtesy of Statesman-Journal

Charles P. Bishop took charge of the one-year-old Salem Woolen Mill Store in 1891. Tailor shop employees made men's clothing early in the new century at 136 Commercial Street. Bishop's Store for Men is now in the Salem Plaza. From Oregon Historical Society/Cronise

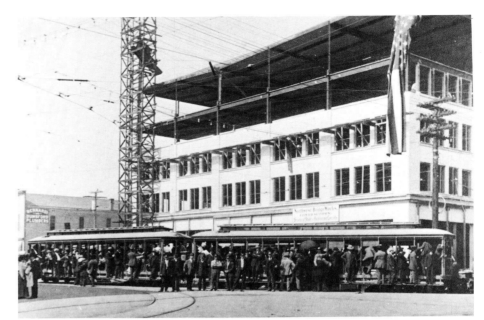

Popular, open-sided Portland streetcars, brought to handle 1909 State Fair crowds, ran beside the partly erected United States Bank of Salem building, housing the Pioneer Trust since 1940. Salem's first steel and concrete bank evolved from the Salem State Bank of 1905 and in 1940 merged with Ladd and Bush Bank. Photograph by Richard Lowenfeld, courtesy of U. S. Bank of Oregon, Ladd and Bush Salem Branch

State Street between 1913 and 1919 had chain stores like Woolworths and a franchised "Painless Parker" dentist (who originated in Salem) along with such local enterprises as the Capitol Drug Store and, since 1912, both T. G. Bligh's Hotel and Theatre. Buildings and businesses along State Street changed little until after World War II. Photograph by June D. Drake, from Oregon Historical Society

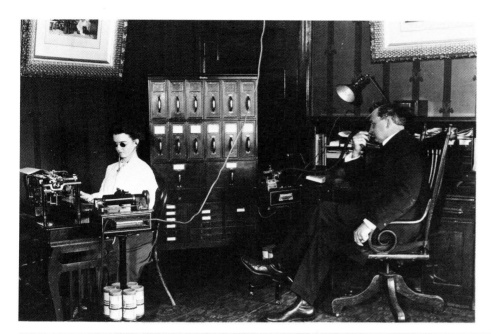

This photograph of a stenographer using a dictating machine in 1914, possibly at the Oregon School for the Blind, indicated that Salem was developing a key urban feature: the creation and spread of information. Courtesy of Oregon State Library/Trover

Fruit and hops became central to Salem's economy in the new century. Marion County later became second nationally only to California's Santa Clara Valley in the volume and variety of its fruit. Here, Salem area children bring in loganberries about 1908. Photograph by George M. Weister, from Oregon Historical Society

Women stood over sloppy floors in a Salem cannery during the 1910s. Salem families labored summers in fields and orchards and in the canneries, fruit drying plants, and packing houses built between 1890 and 1920. From Salem streets, pool halls, cheap hotels, and hobo jungles, "fruit tramps" joined them. Courtesy of Oregon State Library/Trover

Salem strengthened its links to area growers with organizations, services, including improved rail transportation, publicity, and celebrations. Here, men loaded Spitzenburg apple boxes at the tree-shaded Salem depot about 1908. Photograph by George M. Weister, from Oregon Historical Society

The 1908 Cherry Parade passed the Courthouse and Post Office. That year Salem, the Cherry City of the World, greatly expanded the Cherry Festival (or Cherringo), begun in 1903. From a competition for local cherry growers, it became an almost round-the-clock competitive exhibition of fruit plus a parade, dances, sports, and entertainment which soon rivalled July Fourth in importance. Courtesy of Willamette University

Dr. H. H. Schovell was at the controls of the plane he and Ben Taylor modeled on a Curtiss. They failed to get aloft three times at the 1910 State Fair. "First Flight in Salem" title went the next year at the fair to Eugene Ely, a showman who raced cars and motorcycles. Schovell and Taylor then succeeded. Courtesy of Salem Public Library/Maxwell

Under Lincoln's portrait and a Strive and Succeed poster, uniformed Salem Indian Training School students learned history early in the century. The federal school stressed carpentry and other practical skills for those considered unready for reservation life. Students, despite teachers' good intentions, feeling homesick and oppressed, often returned to Pacific Coast reservations. Class, courtesy of Oregon State Library/Trover; shop, courtesy of Willamette University

A crowd watched the Aitchleys around 1914 in the 300 block of State Street. The couple, like many reaching Salem by every possible means of conveyance before and since, also wanted their picture taken before the Capitol and other landmarks or perhaps where free boots were offered by a store having a sale. Photographed by Wesley Andrews, from Oregon Historical Society

Grant School, the last wooden school, opened in 1908 with all eight grades Salem had offered students since 1897. This graceful, easily weathered and broken sidewalk soon gave way to concrete. The present Grant School at 725 Northeast Market Street opened in 1955. Photographed by Howard D. Trover, courtesy of Oregon State Library

Salem's tiny Black population sent one child to this North Salem School class in 1904. From 1868 to the late 1890s, the town officially segregated Black children into the two-room Little Central School, which in 1872 had only fifteen pupils. Courtesy of Salem Public Library/Maxwell

Lai Yick, a respected herbalist, led a Chinese contingent in the 1908 Cherry Fair parade—prompting local Japanese to sponsor a competing float. A recently condemned Chinatown had relocated around South High and Ferry streets with a population consisting mainly of aging bachelors. By 1920, Chinatown was gone. Courtesy of Salem Public Library/Maxwell

A Japanese fraternal association early in the century was decidedly male. A small Japanese community, also embracing Lake Labish farm families, began in the 1900s. It established a Japanese Community Church in 1928. Photograph by Tom Cronise, from Oregon Historical Society/Cronise

The Japanese Hand Laundry and Dry Cleaning Works, 445 Ferry Street, was a family enterprise during World War I. Courtesy of Oregon State Library/Trover

The Hayman Steinbock Junk Company float, at 302-312 North Commercial Street, explained to 1915 Cherry Fair watchers that the Jewish star represents Peace and Liberty. Enough co-religionists by 1919 joined the handful of Jews, present in Salem since the 1860s, to begin active worship services, and in 1947 they established Temple Beth Sholom at 1795 Broadway. From Oregon Historical Society/Cronise

Oregon stored its "insane" in the Insane Asylum, renamed Oregon State Hospital in 1908. "Diagnoses" of brain fever, homesickness, disappointment in love, opium habit, overwork, spiritualism, and religious excitement earned commitment to it during the nineteenth century. When Oregon separated mental retardates in 1908 into what became the Fairview Training Center, the state became more interested in cures than in storage of the mentally ill. Courtesy of Ed Culp

State Penitentiary inmates in 1908 probably liked work on this rock crusher far more than work as leased labor in the prison's Monarch Stove factory, scene of explosions and floggings. Oregon used the crushed rock to macadamize roads. Photograph by Tom Cronise, from Oregon Historical Society/Cronise

May Day Festivals began at Willamette University in 1909 and became all-day affairs. By 1918, the university had survived a bad split in the 1890s, the closing of its pharmacy school and merger of its medical school into the University of Oregon's. It had 223 students in liberal arts, law, and theology programs. Courtesy of Willamette University

This posse and townfolk on Twelfth Street pursued penitentiary escapees Harry Tracy and David Merrill, June 10, 1902. Tracy later killed Merrill and shot himself when surrounded by a posse in eastern Washington. Probably photographed by Walter A. Denton, courtesy of Oregon State Library

Salem has lost three of the four landmarks featured in this popular postcard from the 1900s. The steepled First United Methodist Church, right, built in 1872 on its 1851 site, remains today at Church and State streets the west's oldest Methodist congregation. The Capitol (in farthest background) has burned down, the Courthouse (in foreground) was razed, and the Post Office (in middleground) was moved to become Willamette University's law building. Marble structures replaced all three. Courtesy of Oregon Department of Transportation.

The Breyman brothers gave the city a Spanish-American War statue, Salem's first monument, in 1904. It had water troughs for horses and dogs at the west-end of the Capitol. Although they ordered bronze, they got iron, which later shattered. Only its restored base remains on Cottage Street at the end of Willson Park. Courtesy of Oregon Department of Transportation

A tractor cleaned the twenty-six-inch snow from a Salem streetcar track in December 1919. Occasional heavy snows have never damaged Salem as badly as floods which, today, are controlled by many dams. Courtesy of Frank Cross

The Vaudette Theater, between Steusloff Brothers Meat Market and Capital City Creamery on Court Street, was one of eight silent movie houses in Salem between 1906 and 1908. Courtesy of Salem Public Library/Maxwell

Franklin L. Waters (right) and Harry Moyer (left, in suit) were outside Ye Liberty Theater, 142 North Liberty Street, during a Cherry Fair sometime between 1912 and 1920. Most silent movies charged a nickel and drew crowds from throughout the vicinity. Photograph by Richard Lowenfeld, courtesy of Oregon State Library

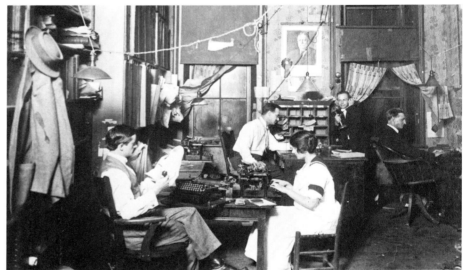

Informal lighting and modern equipment were used in the second floor newsroom of The Oregon Statesman *in 1912, its home at 162½ Northeast Commercial Street for nearly half a century. Under editor-manager Robert J. Hendricks, the daily survived by also publishing farm journals and operating a commercial print and engraving shop. Courtesy of Statesman-Journal*

Governor Oswald West, from Salem, was happy to join sellers of popular magazines on February 17, 1913, before the Capitol. In this era, these magazines often supported political progressives like Oz West. Courtesy of Oregon State Library/Trover

People gathered to await President Roosevelt's arrival in 1903 at a major social center, the Werner Breyman home at State and Cottage streets. Replaced by the Elks Club, the home was moved to 249 Southeast Cottage Street in 1926 and razed in 1975. Since the 1870s Salem has enthusiastically received every president and ex-president and most presidential candidates. Before 1930, however, mostly Republican candidates traveled to heavily Republican Salem. Courtesy of Al Jones

President Theodore Roosevelt (left) and Governor George E. Chamberlain (right) left for a parade on May 21, 1903, after the president spoke to children in Marion Square and from the West Porch of the Capitol. Courtesy of Salem Public Library/Maxwell

Visitors and publicity-seekers alike favored the Capitol as a photographic backdrop. During the 1910s, a Dodge beating its way up the Capitol steps advertised the model's power. Courtesy of Oregon State Library/Trover

Schoolchildren directed by Grace Wheelock, school music supervisor, sang "America" to President William Howard Taft on October 12, 1911, near the Courthouse. Courtesy of Salem Public Library/Maxwell

Dr. James Withycombe's Republican followers in 1902 paraded at the corner of Commercial and Chemeketa streets beneath a banner from the YMCA for George E. Chamberlain, who beat him for governor. Democrat Chamberlain, elected again in 1908, resigned to be twice elected United States Senator; Withycombe won the governor's office in 1914 and again in 1918, just before his death. Courtesy of Oregon State Library/Trover

Woodmen of the World in solemn array with uniforms, swords, and axes in Salem in 1905. The town's numerous fraternal orders by the 1890s originated many of the social activities once found mainly in Salem churches. Photograph by Tom Cronise, from Oregon Historical Society/Cronise

Salem Elks, formed in 1896, wore antlers when visiting fellow Elks in Tacoma, Washington, early in the century. Courtesy of Ed Culp

Housing exhibitors and visitors, a Tent City of tents and wooden shanties at the State Fair had its own streets, events, and traditions. Some 3,000 lived there in 1876, 1,000 in 1900. Autos and trucks doomed it by the 1930s. Courtesy of Oregon State Library/Trover

The serge-suited Cherrians with townfolk and Canadian fliers during the World War I era probably at the State Fair. Organized in 1913, the Cherrians became Salem's most prominent booster organization. They marched at Cherry Fairs and State Fairs, elected annual King Bings, decorated in 1913 the nation's first (they said) Christmas tree, and originated in 1914 a Blossom Day festival, attracting out-of-town visitors to area orchards. Courtesy of Shirley Steeves

Exhibitors lined up at the 1912 Oregon State Fair in front of many long-gone buildings, before they showed, traded, and bought livestock. After some fifty years in Salem, the fair had created strong loyalties and memories among Oregonians. Courtesy of Oregon State Fair

Racing, here at the Lone Oak track, built with a grandstand in 1893, has been a perennial State Fair favorite and source of income. By the 1900s, racing drew trainloads of Portland visitors. Courtesy of Ed Culp

A Hall Grader, manufactured in Marion County, was displayed at the 1910 State Fair. Until the 1930s the fair was mainly designed to interest farmers and farm families. Courtesy of Oregon State Library/Denton

The local Carpenters Union baseball team in the 1900s. The Printers union formed its second Oregon local in Salem in 1888. After American Federation of Labor craft unions became active in Salem between 1902 and 1908, a Salem Trades and Labor Council formed in 1911 to speak for around 400 members. Courtesy of Oregon State Library

Curtis B. Cross stepped carefully along a Silver Creek bridge while hunting during the early 1900s. Until the early 1920s small game and birds abounded at the edge of Salem and in what became Silver Creek State Park. Courtesy of Frank Cross

Cutthroat trout, steelhead, and salmon migrated each spring through Salem streams and ditches, and the Willamette River remained a fine trout stream into the early 1920s. Early in the century, "Fishing on Mill Stream" in Salem involved long poles and getting wet. And fishermen posed in 1910 before Salem Hardware's two-cylinder, sidewinding International delivery truck. Postcard, courtesy of Ed Culp; fishermen, courtesy of Salem Public Library/Maxwell

Children during the 1910s used the Mill Race while others, one with a fashionable Japanese parasol, watched and talked. Neighbors near the river and streams complained if males kept to an old custom and wore no bathing suits. Courtesy of Oregon State Library/Trover

David Eyre, Curtis Cross, Dr. Prince Byrd (tees), Carl Gabrielson, and Frank Spears, Jr. (left to right) played the newly fashionable game of golf at the Illihee Country Club, June 27, 1919. Salem's closest version of a country club opened near South River Road for golf and picnics in a log club house in 1914. Today's newer Illahee Hills Country Club, greens, and clubhouse, are just to the north. Courtesy of Frank Cross

In 1903 and later years, the Old Gaiety Dance Club and similar private Salem groups were popular with wealthier families. Photograph by Cronise Studio; courtesy of U. S. Bank of Oregon, Ladd and Bush Salem Branch

Bridge and garden parties, some displaying interest in Asia, were the most stylish entertainments before World War I. Some of these prominent women in 1910 organized the Salem Women's Club, which expanded women's interest into new cultural and civic realms. Women like these founded the first public library in 1912 and the YWCA in 1913. Like earlier temperance and church leagues, these activities helped women recognize their potential power in collective action. Courtesy of Oregon State Library/Trover

Until the mid-1920s children from wealthier families enrolled in private dancing schools, where they sometimes performed. Courtesy of Mary Minto

W. M. Derrick and friends, in October 1907, continued the pioneer tradition of homemade music. Lively amateur music, including yearly contests at the State Fair, long marked Salem's homes, clubs, and regular public calendar. Photograph by Tom Cronise, from Oregon Historical Society/ Cronise

Most in the Salem vicinity watched a spontaneous victory parade march west on Court Street on November 11, 1918. Salem men in the 3rd Oregon Infantry had gone to France in December 1917 and returned from World War I to great fanfare in February 1919. Postcard courtesy of Frank Cross

The thirty-four-member Salem Symphony Orchestra, under Professor John Sites of Willamette University, began in 1919 in the showcase Grand Opera House in the Odd Fellows Hall. It later played in the Salem Armory, erected in 1912. It became the Salem Philharmonic in 1935, playing until 1942 in high school auditoriums and also in Willamette Valley May Festivals. Courtesy of Oregon State Library/Trover

Chapter Four

1920–1940

The new Oregon Pulp and Paper Company plant in 1920, pictured in the 1930s, the Western Paper Company in 1926 and new and bigger food and fiber processing firms added up to real industrial growth for Salem during the 1920s. By the early 1930s, the expanded paper mill meant valuable jobs as well as unpleasant smells and cinders and added pollution to the Willamette River. Photograph by Salem Flying Service; courtesy of Boise Cascade Paper Group, Salem, Oregon

The Circuit Rider, erected on Capitol grounds in 1924, paid tribute to the Reverend Robert A. Booth, a Methodist minister in the 1850s, and to other ministers and missionaries who spread religion in the pioneer Oregon settlements. Courtesy of Oregon Department of Transportation

In Salem, 1920 found the Oregon Pulp and Paper Company producing Salem's first paper. The Western Paper Converting Company followed in 1926. Paper was a very appropriate item for the city. As state capital and home to numerous state institutions, Salem used reams of it, more after the Depression imposed new governmental responsibilities. As a thriving regional supplier, it sold paper products to farms and villages. As an expanding center in the 1920s for canners, packers and linen mills, it used larger amounts of it. A small city with offices, newspapers, farm publications, and other information providers—it needed still more paper. And so did a population which jumped from 17,679 to 30,908 between 1920 and 1940.

Cars and trucks were closely associated with these Salem industries and purposes. Motorized vehicles quickened changes in Salem's shape, patterns, and activities. Service stations, supermarkets, chain stores, and other firms—all oriented to cars and trucks—multiplied. The fire department motorized early in the 1920s. Buses replaced the last trolleys in 1927. Cars enabled the Hollywood district to offer, in the 1920s, Salem's first shopping outside downtown. Trucking turned businesses away from the river, and commercial traffic on the Willamette almost ended by the mid-1930s.

A small building boom (mainly in housing), underway in 1923, could ignore streetcars and build on outskirts reachable by autos. Wealthier people moved onto hillsides roughly south of State and west of Winter streets. Some took improved roads to Portland but many more came into Salem from smaller places for shopping, selling, and entertainment. Auto-borne visitors could stay in a new municipal campground or, as late as the 1940s, in Pringle Park. Tent City was no longer needed at the fairgrounds. The city adopted planning and zoning in 1926.

Salem happily adopted or expanded city ways and institutions between the world wars. Movie "palaces," neighborhood theaters, and radio stations opened. Local drama groups came and went. The Salem Senators played semi-professional baseball; Miller's Department Store offered big city fashions. The Crystal Gardens Ballroom promised

"two floors, two bands, for two bits." In 1926, Parrish, the first junior high school, opened, as did the eleven-story First National Bank, which, as the Capitol Tower, remains Salem's skyscraper. The city acquired an airport, a new post office, dial phones, traffic signals, more concrete sidewalks, and more paved streets.

Salem worried about pastimes which kept people from home or church. Prohibition laws before 1934 did not halt beer and liquor consumption. Residents did stop drinking greenish, bad-tasting water from the Willamette. The city bought the water company and, after 1937, drew instead from the clean Santiam River. The Willamette was left to users not bothered by its untreated sewage and industrial wastes.

Familiar, even small-town, ways persisted. Families, churches, and clubs furnished centers and guidance through the prospering 1920s and difficult 1930s. Church edifices grew more prominent. The First Presbyterian Church enlarged its building for a growing membership; Catholics opened a second school and church, St. Vincent de Paul. Fraternal organizations became more numerous and active. The YMCA ran a big church baseball league. Town leaders praised women and children each summer for helping to bring in crops and for working in canneries and packing houses.

Salem remained small enough for walking—a necessity for the poor—and close enough to nature in the 1920s for windmills to exist and for coyotes to raid chicken coops. Strollers on warm evenings stopped to hear voices or music issuing through open windows or to join front porch sitters. Salem now had a municipal band in Willson Park, a fretted string orchestra, an American Legion Drum Corp, a symphony, and the MacDowell Club chorus.

Merchants liked to consider themselves "go getters" but usually opened shops at noon. Though reporters no longer waited at the depot to gather news of visits, Colonel Charles A. Lindbergh's low flight over the city drew large crowds and big headlines.

Local boosters, well into the 1940s, sought to attract out-of-state farmers to settle among "100 percent Americans" with "absolutely no foreign element." Even the small Chinatown disappeared during the 1920s. That Salem was overwhelmingly white and native-born (and keen on morality) was insufficient early in the 1920s for the Ku Klux Klan. Before folding, the Klan baited Catholics mainly with words. Few other than George Putnam's *Capital Journal* publicly opposed the Klan. Putnam also fought prohibition and local gamblers; in the 1930s, he fought union organizing. At *The Oregon Statesman* Charles Sprague was midway in a forty-year career as editor, interrupted in 1939 for one term as governor.

A Salem that was frugal, close to the land, and dependent on no single employer endured the national Depression better than did many small cities. In fact, some midwestern and southern farmers came to Marion County. Salem actually added more people than did Portland during the

Statues recall both Salem's pioneers and its war dead. The Doughboy, dedicated early in the 1920s, rises above today's Marion Square to honor men killed during the First World War. Photograph by Gerry Lewin, courtesy of Statesman-Journal

1930s. Fred Meyer and Sears and Roebuck thought it profitable to open Salem stores early in the Depression. Residents also experienced job losses, shorter hours, lowered pay, and fear of worsening times. Cannery work paid thirty-eight cents an hour, and forty other workers waited to replace each employee. Proud workers took public jobs, paid for mainly with federal funds, to build the first public swimming pools, improve parks and playing fields, and erect state buildings. The Capitol, stunningly lost in a 1935 fire, was replaced in 1938.

Cultural affairs flowered under private and governmental auspices during the Depression. The YMCA organized a Twilight University and various cultural programs. A Community Concert Association was formed. The Salem Federal Arts Center encouraged local talent. These actions partly offset Portland's cultural drawing power. Despite adversity, Salem by 1940 had struggled, often successfully, to retain its strengths as a community and important regional center.

The Motor Shop operated two shops late in the 1920s and closed at 255 North Church Street in 1933. It was one of many new firms serving Salem's growing car and truck population between the two wars. And it suffered the Depression-fate of many small businesses. Courtesy of Oregon State Library/Trover

The automobile helped transform small neighborhood markets into supermarkets, some of which organized into chains. This was the history of Skaggs, which at 162 and 270 North Commercial Street late in the 1920s became part of the early Safeway chain. Courtesy of Oregon State Library/Trover

In 1919 Salem busily paved neighborhood streets and changed downtown topography by filling, grading, and paving. With thirty-five miles of paved streets in 1923, and many cement walks since 1905, Salem planned further big city improvements. Courtesy of Oregon State Library/Trover

The Hollywood business district replaced wheat and cherry growers to become in the 1920s Salem's first shopping area outside downtown. By the 1930s, small, service-oriented businesses lined the 1900 block of Capitol Street. This open-fronted Safeway sold hamburger for fifteen cents a pound. Photograph by Wesley Andrews, postcard from Oregon Historical Society/Andrews

In 1921 Gideon Stolz Company, a former brewery on South Summer Street between Mill and Bellvue streets, made apple cider vinegar and bottled soft drinks. The 1879 firm later became a beer distributor. Courtesy of Oregon State Library/Trover

Salem was more important as a food and fiber processor between the world wars than in earlier periods. Clifford W. Brown as a broker during the 1920s conducted a mohair warehouse at 171 Front Street and separate warehouses for hops and wool. Meanwhile, new and bigger canneries and packers serviced fruit and vegetable growers; Valley Packing Company, meat interests. Courtesy of Oregon State Library/Trover

Oregon Flax Textile Company, opened in 1943, was destined to be the last of a local industry dating from the 1860s. During the 1920s the new Miles Linen Company and the Oregon Linen Mill (later Salem Linen Mills) expanded flax processing in Salem. Workers at Oregon Flax Textile produced rug backing at its 859 Seventh Street plant not long before its 1956 closing. Courtesy of McEwan Photo Studios

Here, an Oregon Stages coach is in Salem in the late 1920s; it was acquired and renamed Oregon Motor Stages in the 1930s by the Southern Pacific Railroad. Locally, Thomas E. McLean in 1921 had begun a "jitney" bus, charging a nickel for a ride in Salem. In 1927 the last trolleys gave way to buses. Courtesy of Oregon State Library/Trover

These planes stood at Salem Airport, later McNary Field, in 1931. The local American Legion chapter spearheaded its development; Lee Eyerly was its first manager. Courtesy of Frank Hrubetz

Lee Eyerly ran a pilot school; also, he designed and built airplanes before beginning Salem's amusement ride industry in 1931. The "Aeroplane" of 1931 was one of fifty developed from an unsuccessful pilot training device; it rotated in three planes but had an overly difficult access by ladder to the cockpit. Courtesy of Frank Hrubetz

The Clean Teeth Transportation Company of Englewood School first graders, about 1929, showed the influence both of Salem's new airport and four years of county-wide health demonstrations, financed by New York's The Commonwealth Fund due to Chamber of Commerce initiative. The process led to the establishment of the Marion County Health Department. Courtesy of The Commonwealth Fund

Northern access to the city, on the Pacific Highway, came through a needed underpass beside the Valley Packing Company, near the fairgrounds in 1936. Salem still complained that railroad tracks interfered with vehicle traffic and worked against residential and industrial development. Courtesy of Oregon State Library/WPA

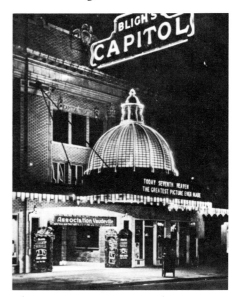

Salem's first movie palaces opened in 1926. Bligh's Capitol seated 1,200 and later lost its State Street cupola; the Elsinore, graced by Shakespearian murals, seated 1,400 at 170 Southeast High Street. Both had live productions and movies, first silent ones. Courtesy of Statesman-Journal

In 1922 the Cherringo, in the Salem Armory Auditorium, was the last Cherry Fair event held until there was a brief revival between 1947 and 1954. The Cherrians continued to elect a member King Bing each year. Courtesy of Frank Cross

Kids crowded Saturday matinees at the Grand Theater, 193 North High Street, where emcee Zollie Volchok's Zollie's Gang presided during talent shows. The Capitol and Elsinore also had popular matinees during the 1930s. Courtesy of Oregon State Library/Trover

People enjoyed a slide and diving board during the late 1920s (probably into Mill Creek near what became the airport). A pond formed by the Oregon Pulp and Paper Mill dam in the early 1920s also became popular; bath houses and concession stands for it were along State Street. It is now Mill Race Park at Northeast Twenty-First and Ferry streets. Courtesy of Oregon State Library/Trover

Salmon fishing along North Mill Creek near Church Street on May 27, 1928, was good. However, by then orchards replacing grain farms plus improved roads, bringing hunters from elsewhere, made game scarcer around Salem. Courtesy of Mission Mill Museum Association

The sternwheeler Relief from Portland was caught at the foot of Court Street, December 29, 1924, as drifting ice filled the river from shore to shore. Local interests conducted the Salem Navigation Company, later a trucking company, from 1927 to 1934. Afterwards, the Depression, higher stevedoring costs, and heavy truck traffic throughout the Valley almost stopped the river traffic. Courtesy of Salem Public Library/Maxwell

A caning class between the wars used the basement at the Oregon School for the Blind, opened in 1873. Students, in a school now serving the multi-handicapped, also learned piano tuning and other trades. Courtesy of Oregon School for the Blind

Circus parades, such as this one in 1922, beckoned patrons and local help several times a year. Salem itself between 1909 and World War II was home to the Browning Brothers Amusement Company, which conducted carnival shows throughout the region. Courtesy of Ed Culp

Oregon's pioneering workmen's compensation law gave injured workers access, in Salem and Portland, to physiotherapy to help regain use of their limbs. In 1922, they used mechanical apparatuses. From State Industrial Accident Commission Report (Salem, 1922)

Salem's Fraternal Order of Eagles joined other groups pressing for old age pensions sometime before the Roosevelt Administration and Congress established the Social Security System in the 1930s. Courtesy of Oregon State Library/Trover

Fire on April 25, 1935, reduced the State Capitol. Crowds watched into the night and gathered, still stunned, at the ruins on following days. Oregon opened its present Capitol and separate State Library in 1938. Loss of the old Capitol remained Salem's most traumatic single event and apparently influenced many in the 1950s and 1960s to believe that Salem should build anew, not save old buildings. Courtesy of Oregon State Library

Oregon Workers Alliance members protested a Senate old age pension bill in front of the Marion Hotel, the temporary Capitol, March 5, 1936. Salem was scene to various Depression and postwar marches and protests. Union organizing had made little headway in Salem by 1939, however. From Oregon Historical Society/Oregon Journal

The Hotel De Minto, named for police chief Frank Minto, who arranged the lodging in the empty old Armory atop City Hall, sheltered destitutes in 1938. Mostly young, they chopped wood and performed other tasks for hash and stew, heat from oil drums, and rest on old army cots. Courtesy of Salem Public Library/Maxwell

Most of Salem, including those in the bookkeeping department of the Ladd and Bush Bank in 1939, kept their jobs during the Depression. Many faced shorter hours and low pay. Barter, home gardens, habits of frugality, aid from farm relatives, and governmental relief and jobs all helped many to survive the hard years. Courtesy of U. S. National Bank of Oregon, Ladd and Bush Salem Branch

Chapter Five

1940–1960

A 1947 photograph taken from the windows of the Goodyear Blimp showed downtown, log rafts in the river, the slough, and the busy paper mill. Major changes were taking place in Salem. Courtesy of Salem Public Library/Maxwell

Salem answered the national call for scrap aluminum by collecting vast heaps on the Courthouse lawn on July 30, 1941. The country was rearming and aiding the Allies before entering World War II. Courtesy of Salem Public Library/Maxwell

The Salem Centennial in 1940 celebrated remaining links to Salem's pioneer past and noted its progress during the first hundred years of town existence. Many families and institutions traced their ancestry to the early village. Many structures from past eras remained in use. Centennial costumes, old fire equipment, and frontier contests further reminded Salem of the living past. The present was also on citizens' minds: the Depression lingered; also, officially neutral America was becoming involved in the war raging abroad.

Volunteering, an old Salem tradition, was common once war came. Salemites volunteered for military service and for bond, blood, and scrap drives. They helped house and entertain the thousands of soldiers, some with families, stationed in 1943 and 1944 at Camp Adair, hastily built near the Marion County line. Willamette University, losing its male students, volunteered to replace them with navy recruits from the nation's speeded-up V-12 education program. Volunteers joined in as Salem, and especially West Salem, battled a bad flood in 1943.

War made local industry and Oregon agriculture boom. Mills worked overtime and the flax industry expanded. The work force began unionizing at the busy canners and packers. Local unions erected a Labor Temple. Because they had access to nearby farms, Salemites managed to obtain rationed food although other articles were scarce. The flow of jobs and money brought heady experiences after the difficult years of Depression. But Salem's Japanese-Americans experienced none of this. In 1942 they and other West Coast Japanese-Americans were swept into internment camps.

A population jump of almost 40 percent in the 1940s, though this was only moderate compared to other Oregon cities, spelled growing pains for Salem. Difficulties mounted during the rush into peacetime. Everyone seemed to want the jobs and the housing and the products, cars especially, denied by Depression and war. Construction exploded into the fertile vegetable, fruit, and grain areas around Salem. Housing and businesses spread in Polk County and south and east into hills around town. The metropolitan area became the "real" city as people increasingly lived and maintained economic and cultural institutions both outside and inside Salem boundaries.

Salem's postwar downtown deteriorated. Sulfurous odors from the paper mill penetrated homes near it. Many downtown buildings had been so neglected that some people would bet which old store would cave in first. Downtown was choked by too many bridges and busy rail crossings and by traffic running through on Highway 99. Parking became easier in suburban shopping

districts that sprang up in the 1950s and 1960s.

However, fresh local enterprise answered what might have turned into a longterm decline for the city. These initiatives were rooted in its citizens' considerable loyalty to Salem, their respect for its many attractive features, their pride in its institutions. Salem had the state's, and in one published appraisal, the nation's best public schools. And its state capital status guaranteed it would never become just a way station on the highway.

An important Long Range Planning Commission began encouraging intelligent development and the cooperation of unincorporated areas. The city modernized in 1947 with a City Manager-Council form of government. It also improved and extended crucial utilities: a new sewage system in 1952; natural gas connection in 1956; and water, that decade, from the North Santiam River above Stayton flowed into city mains. Two hundred volunteers began in 1956 to study ways to integrate and improve area-wide public services. When the bus company went bankrupt in 1958, employees took it over; then, in 1966, the city. Yet, the new Marion Street Bridge, erected in 1952, and an improved Center Street Bridge still proved inadequate for increasing cross-river traffic. Meanwhile, the Willamette River remained heavily polluted.

From 1946 to 1960 the city also annexed thirty-one sections, and more incorporations followed. The annexation of West Salem in 1949 gave Salem an unusual two-county city administration plus a population spurt. Still, the overall metropolitan area grew faster than Salem. During the 1950s, Eugene, for the first time in history, passed Salem as Oregon's second largest city. Salem added about 6,000 people in that decade, only about 1,300 more than during the Depression years.

Salem earned its living in new ways by the 1950s. Marion County became far more of a service center than it had been in earlier eras. It became a center for finance, insurance (new regional offices of Allstate and State Farm Mutual), and real estate. Governmental employment grew as did trade. Meier and Frank, Lipman's (now Frederick and Nelson), Newberry, Grants, and other chain stores built downtown. This shifted the commercial hub, drove out some older businesses such as Miller's, and attracted others. Downtown revitalization took a new turn with the new stores and offices. Paper production flourished, and Moore Business Forms located in Salem.

Regional agriculture shifting toward more vegetables than fruit meant postwar changes in Salem's important processing industry. Freezing operations were also added, and these offered some year-round employment for the seasonal industry. By 1956 unions represented its workforce as well as many in the thriving construction industry. In the fifties, Salem lost some familiar industries. The last flax mill closed in 1956; the Thomas Kay Woolen Mill stopped manufacturing in 1958. The Alumina plant, not opened until after the war, attracted few tenants and was finally razed.

Beards, parades, a pageant, and pioneer contests sprouted during the Salem Centennial. The city displayed old handpumpers and steam engines beside newer equipment. Courtesy of Salem Public Library/ Maxwell

The Centennial was the major event of 1940. For several glorious summer days and evenings thousands celebrated a recreated pioneer past and progress made over the past hundred years. Costumed Salemites visited pioneer facades along Court Street. Courtesy of Salem Public Library/ Maxwell

Salem kept its old liking for urban ways and civic improvements. New homes and buildings had to have the most modern conveniences. There had to be new schools, including South Salem as a second high school, for a growing population. Willamette Univeristy set out on a major postwar campaign of improvement and expansion. The Pentacle Theater started with an experimental theater in a barn west of town. Bush Pasture's Park opened. Wallace Marine Park in West Salem offered new picnic facilities and boat launching ramps. The Cherryland Festival, from 1947 to 1951, tried to revive the Cherry Festival traditions. The Salem Art Association's postwar revival proved successful.

Salem also tore down many of the old homes and stores which gave genuine evidence of its pioneer or Victorian past. Little was preserved beyond Bush House, opening in 1953. In the name of progess, new buildings replaced the tumbledown ones, reminders of the nineteenth century industry and transportation along Trade and Front streets. The state weighed in with Public Service and Highway buildings designed for up-to-date efficiency. Statues erected to the Reverend Jason Lee, Dr. John McLoughlin, and to the pioneers offered symbols, but less substance remained of the past.

During the Salem Centennial, a Wilkie-McNary float boosted Salem's most illustrious son, Senator and Republican vice-presidential nominee Charles McNary, against Roosevelt and Wallace in the forthcoming 1940 election. Courtesy of Salem Public Library/Maxwell

In 1941 the Senators played their second season of professional ball at George Waters Field. The stadium, which opened on Southeast Twenty-Fifth Street in 1940 to a record-setting crowd of 4,865, burned down in 1961. The team did not play during World War II; however, from 1960 to 1965 they played as the Dodgers. In 1977 the Senators began pro ball again. Photograph by Kennell-Ellis Studio; courtesy of Al Jones

The possibility of entering another world war was much on Salem's mind as residents gathered for Memorial Day beside the river in 1940. They had many reminders of past wars: Civil War veterans paraded until 1939, and uniformed Spanish-American War and World War I veterans still appeared in Salem parades. Courtesy of Salem Public Library/Maxwell

The first airmail left Salem on December 5, 1941, two days before the Pearl Harbor attack. From left to right: Postal Messenger Harry Patton, Postmaster Henry R. Crawford, Armond Garrett, and Airmail Superintendent A. O. Willoughby loaded a United Air Lines plane. Courtesy of Salem Public Library/Maxwell

A hundred thousand troops were at Camp Adair in 1943 and 1944. Troops were often seen at the Salem depot. Courtesy of Ed Culp

Relaxing in 1943 at the U. S. O. in the former Unitarian Church on High Street. Volunteers converted and staffed gyms, church halls, and old stores and guided and entertained soldiers to make them feel more at home in Salem. Courtesy of McEwan Photo Shops

A Salem Safeway store on May 16, 1944, reminded shoppers that prices remained reasonable. Federal price control was mandated nationally. Courtesy of McEwan Photo Shops

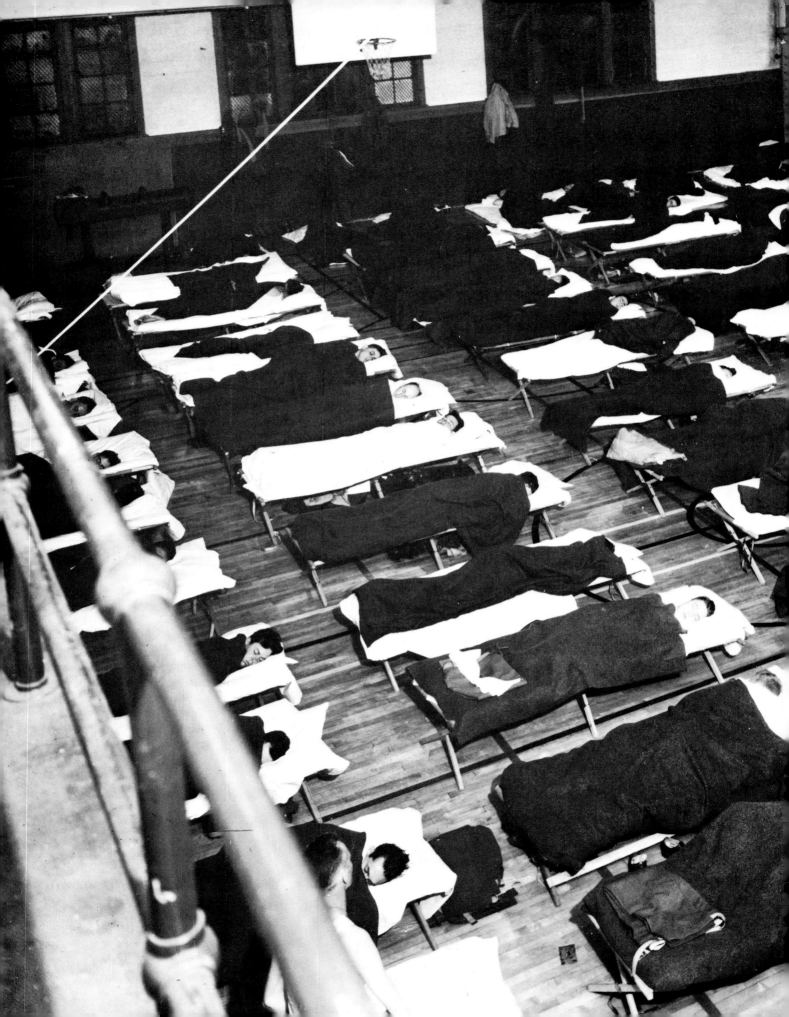

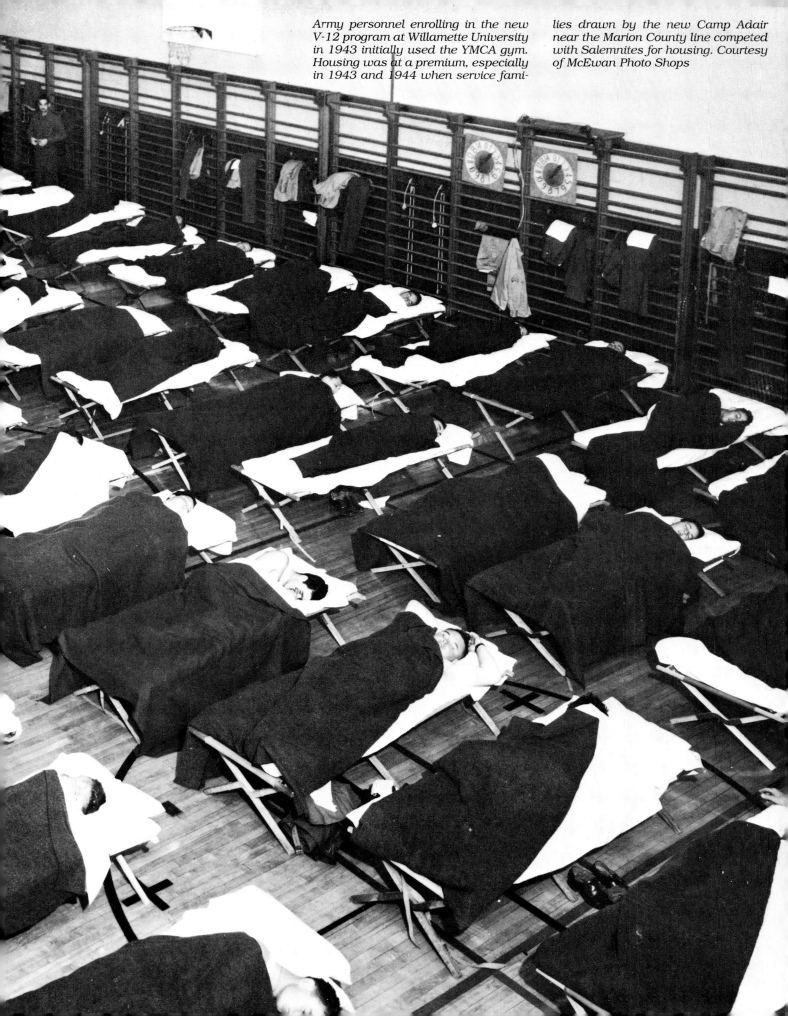

Army personnel enrolling in the new V-12 program at Willamette University in 1943 initially used the YMCA gym. Housing was at a premium, especially in 1943 and 1944 when service families drawn by the new Camp Adair near the Marion County line competed with Salemnites for housing. Courtesy of McEwan Photo Shops

In July 1942 "Scrappo" overlooked the Courthouse lawn during one of the many wartime drives. Meanwhile, Salem strained to meet its wartime needs as its industry and agricultural processing, and with these, jobs, expanded. Courtesy of Salem Public Library/Maxwell

Curly's Dairy, now at 2310 Southeast Mission Street, did the practical and patriotic thing when faced by wartime scarcities. Courtesy of Ed Culp

Once rationing ended and consumer production began again, Salem joined in the buying spree. Shoppers lined up to buy nylons at Miller's Department Store, April 11, 1946. Courtesy of Salem Public Library/ Maxwell

Bells, whistles, sirens, and horns brought V-J celebrants laughing and weeping into streets at war's end on August 14, 1945. *Courtesy of Salem Public Library/Maxwell*

State Street looking eastward in the mid-1940s had antiquated buses and elderly buildings grown shabby or worse. A 1947 national survey said that Salem was one of the poorest places to shop in the United States. *Courtesy of* Statesman-Journal

The alumina plant, not completed until after the war, became a white elephant containing only a short-lived fertilizer plant and research operations. It was razed in 1955-1956 after efforts to find other occupants failed. Courtesy of Statesman-Journal

The Joseph Holman Building housed Oregon's state legislature and offices above stores at Commercial and Ferry streets from 1859 to 1876. A two-story wing added in 1866 contained the town's first theater.

A parking structure has replaced the building, razed in 1951, here pictured in 1949. Courtesy of Oregon State Library

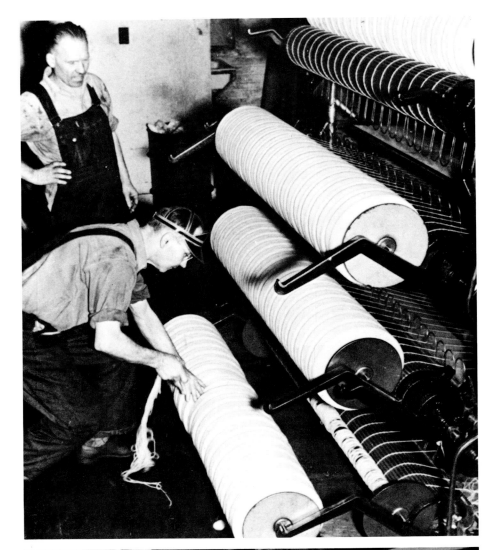

Don Sharff looked on as George North removed a row of "roving" from the carder before the Thomas Kay Wollen Mill spun it in 1947. Manufacturing there ended in 1958, and the dying plant closed in 1962. The company became a carpet retailer; the buildings, the core of the Mission Mill Museum, are now being restored. Courtesy of Mission Mill Museum Association

Women filled cans of green beans at Paulus Brothers, acquired in 1955 by Dole, which as Castle and Cooke Foods closed the plant in 1982. The Salem area processed about one quarter of the Pacific Northwest fruit and vegetables in 1957. Photograph by Kennel-Ellis Studio, courtesy of Castle and Cooke Foods

After Frank Hrubetz left Lee Eyerly's factory, he manufactured wartime products, then built his own amusement rides, including this Number One Round Up for Jantzen Beach in Portland in 1953. Courtesy of Frank Hrubetz

Linotype operators worked in The Oregon Statesman's *new plant in the 1950s. Ex-governor Charles A. Sprague's paper had become a seven-day-a-week publication to fight heavy inroads made by* The Oregonian *from Portland in its Salem readership. Then, retailers new to the downtown in the mid- and late-1950s boosted the* Statesman *and the* Capital Journal *with advertising in order to reach their mid-Willamette Valley audiences. Courtesy of Salem Area Chamber of Commerce*

Station K.O.C.O. beamed radio programs from 1426 Edgewater in West Salem from the mid-1940s to the mid-1950s. In 1947 Margaret Pickett and Dave Hoss seemed very relaxed as they broadcast. Courtesy of McEwan Photo Shops

In 1952 Clare Painter used earphones and lip reading to teach Oregon State School for the Deaf students correct speech pronunciation. Today, children born deaf use individual hearing aids but still need the same determination and effort to acquire language. Courtesy of Oregon State School for the Deaf

The Salem City Band performed evenings in 1946 in this Marion Square Bandstand. Willson Park had popular Saturday evening band concerts after 1948. Courtesy of U. S. Bank of Oregon, Ladd and Bush Salem Branch

In 1947 Salem Federated Musicians performed at Mayor Robert L. Elfstrom's home, 125 West Lincoln Street, now the residence of Willamette University presidents. A revival of serious music, after wartime disbanding of the Symphony, included a Junior Symphony in 1953 and, in 1964, the Willamette University-Salem Community Symphony, forerunner of the present Salem Symphony. Courtesy of McEwan Photo Studios

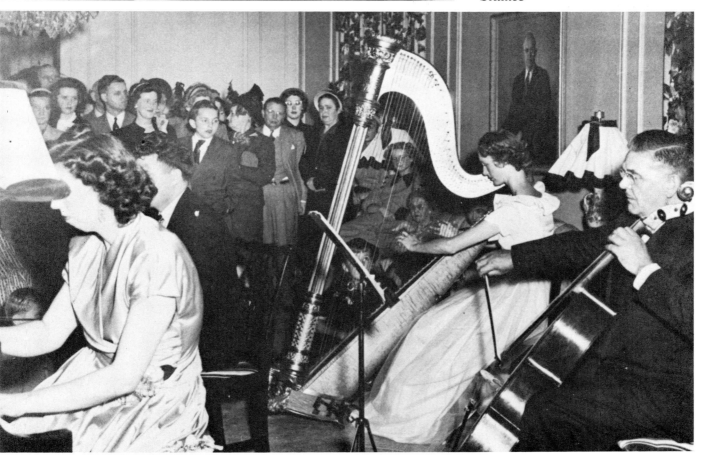

Willamette University engaged in a major postwar campaign of improvements and expansion. McCulloch Stadium was built in 1950 for football, replacing Sweetland Field with its leaky roof and grounds of dust or mud. Courtesy of Salem Area Chamber of Commerce

The 1923 gym was used February 12, 1954, when the Bearcats lost unexpectedly 68 to 60 to Pacific University's Badgers. Willamette University recreation and physical education moved to the new Sparks Center in 1974, and the old gym was renovated into a theater. Courtesy of McEwan Photo Studios

After the wartime shutdown, the shabby State Fair—every major building had been condemned in 1935—continued its policy, begun in the 1930s, to add new programs to widen its base from rural and small-town Oregon. Aiming at year-round use, it also offered by the 1950s space for conventions and their art shows. Courtesy of Salem Area Chamber of Commerce

Horse racing in 1955 remained a perennial favorite of fairgoers. Photograph by John Erickson; from Oregon Historical Society/Oregon Journal

Downtown retailers briefly promoted a Children's Balloon Parade in the mid-1950s to attract post-Thanksgiving shoppers from the multiplying suburban shopping areas or to prevent them from driving to Portland. Here, the 1958 parade is at State and High streets. Courtesy of Statesman-Journal

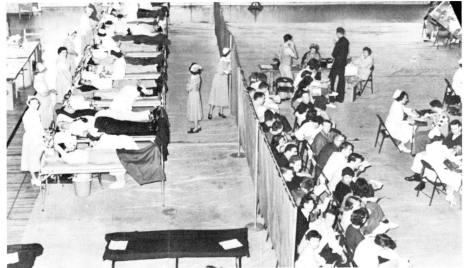

During the Korean War, like many times before and since, Salem residents contributed blood to the Red Cross. Courtesy of Salem/Oregon Statesman

The House of Representatives met in 1947 in this building, then ample for Oregon's government needs. Discussion began twenty years later about whether the governor and the legislature needed greater space, and in 1976 two wings were added behind the Capitol. Courtesy of Oregon State Library

Governor Douglas McKay joined presidential candidate Dwight Eisenhower's fifteen-minute campaign stop on October 7, 1952, attracting the largest depot crowd remembered in Salem. McKay, onetime Salem auto dealer and mayor, became Eisenhower's Secretary of the Interior in 1953. Courtesy of Al Jones

Numerous buildings etched in Salem memories came down during the 1950s and 1960s. Salem High School on Northeast Marion Street, Salem's sole high school from 1906 to 1917, appeared solidly permanent a year before its 1954 replacement by the Meier and Frank Department Store, which retained the trees. Courtesy of Salem Public Library/Maxwell

Ashael Bush II, founder of The Oregon Statesman and the Ladd and Bush Bank and a power in Oregon until his 1913 death, built this simplified Victorian mansion in 1877-1878. There were also a greenhouse, barn (replaced after a 1963 fire), and pastured cattle on the sizeable estate. Bush House, also the residence of his daughter Sally Bush and then of his banker son A. N. Bush, has been open to the public since 1953 at 600 Southeast Mission Street. Courtesy of Al Jones

Salem's outdoor, illuminated Christmas tree was planted by the Cherrians in 1913. It is pictured here at the Marion County Courthouse in 1949, five years before the structure was replaced. The Christmas tree tradition did not survive afterward at the Post Office. Courtesy of Statesman-Journal

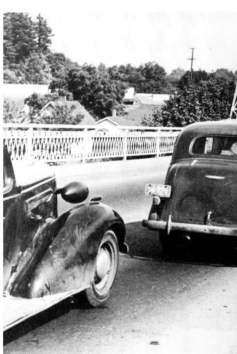

A train loaded with logs blocked the Center Street Bridge into Salem in 1942. Salem at war's end began planning to deal with tracks blocking four sides of the business district, with

The ornate west facade of Washington School, built in the 1880s as East Salem School, was still beautiful not long before its 1949 supplanting by a Safeway store at Center and Twelfth streets. Photograph by Ben Maxwell, courtesy of Oregon State Library

thirty-seven bridges between it and neighborhoods, and with train switching which disturbed residents' sleep. Courtesy of Salem Area Chamber of Commerce

A crane lifted a section of the Marion Street Bridge, which opened December 14, 1952. The inadequate two-lane Center Street Bridge was then improved. Courtesy of the City of Salem/Oregon Statesman

In 1943, the Willamette River peaked on January first and second after nearly sixty days of precipitation. West Salem, hardest hit, had wave-like flooding while, at the Wallace Road junction, a car and buildings were awash from the thirty-foot high river. Two city workmen died trying to dislodge the old Mellow Moon Dance Hall from a Center Street Bridge approach. Courtesy of Salem Public Library/Maxwell

The Monticello *dredged the river in vain hopes of restoring serious river traffic to Salem early in the 1950s. Courtesy of* Salem/Oregon Statesman

A close-up of the Oregon Pulp and Paper Company, probably about 1955, showed its river waste and air pollution. Acquired by Boise Cascade in 1962, the company began to put waste into a lagoon. Under growing state and local pressure, it made further expensive, successful advances against water and air pollution. Courtesy of Statesman-Journal

This was part of West Salem in 1959, a decade after its annexation to Salem. Growth continued on both sides of the river. Photograph by John Ericksen, courtesy of Statesman-Journal

Rustic sites and views abounded even as Salem grew more urban and metropolitan after World War II. The North Mill Creek footbridge was near the Willamette River in 1953. Courtesy of Salem Public Library/Maxwell

Chapter Six

1960–1980

Two hundred volunteers had begun in 1956 to study ways for Salem, Marion and Polk counties, the state, and area schools to improve and integrate their operations. Many of the volunteers' preventive proposals resulted in beneficial cooperative arrangements on port development, parks, sewage disposal, and other public needs. The Salem area won a coveted "All America City" award in 1961 for the effort. Here, Mayor Russell Bonesteele (behind banner), Chamber of Commerce President (and ex-mayor) Willard Marshall (left) and an honor guard ready the banner announcing All-America Salem in March 1961. From Oregon Historical Society/Oregon Journal

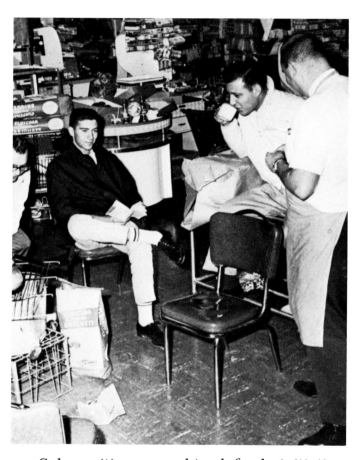

During a blackout brought on by the Columbus Day Storm, supermarket employees made coffee and hot dogs on a charcoal broiler. Courtesy of Statesman-Journal

Salem citizens combined fresh initiatives with tested ways in confronting change during the 1960s and 1970s, just as they had in the past. The Salem area won a coveted national All America City award in 1961 for five years' cooperation among governments and schools. This cooperation had triggered important preventive actions concerning development and public services, such as park development. No resting on laurels followed the award. The metropolitan region still strained under the weight of new people, new structures, new demands.

Growth of state government and facilities during these decades brought advantages in the form of new buildings and bigger payrolls. The growing population remained overwhelmingly native-born and white, though there were increasing numbers of blacks and Hispanics. More people meant more houses, stores, and churches. They also meant congested schools and overloaded public services. Absentee ownership of Salem enterprises increased, too. Larger concerns could make valuable improvements in the major processors, the paper mill, and the stores. However, key decisions about their and Salem's future thereafter happened at a distance.

The completion of Interstate 5 in 1961 made metropolitan Portland, spreading toward Salem, a more threatening presence than ever. Yet, easier highway access fortunately helped maintain Salem as a regional trade and service center. Valley agricultural riches still came to Salem. In the 1960s and 1970s the sprouting hamlets and unincorporated areas, almost alone, forced Salem to choose revitalization—rather than decline.

By untangling its streets, removing track along Union Street (in 1980, along Trade Street, too), opening new offices and stores, and beginning a paper mill cleanup, Salem made its downtown more welcoming in the 1960s. Through aggressive annexation and offers of needed public services, it incorporated adjacent districts. Taking in the large South Salem area in 1964 boosted the population from over 50,000 to almost 63,000. Further annexation and growth brought Salem's population to over 89,000 people in 1980, with around 237,000 in the total metropolitan region.

An enlarged Capitol with new city, state, and county buildings, and new commercial structures stretched the downtown district. Salem beautified

downtown by uncovering streams once hidden beneath streets and behind factories. The city spread fine new parks, plazas, cascading pools, footpaths, and bicycle ways through it; also, it greatly expanded parks and other recreational facilities. Better city sewage and paper mill waste treatment improved Salem's water and atmosphere. Municipal and industrial cleanups all along its banks made the Willamette again fit for fishing and swimming. The salmon had returned by the late 1970s.

Private and public funds went to revitalize inner city neighborhoods and the growth zones on Salem's fringes. Neighborhood associations formed to affect these and then other decisions. Private volunteers and companies started to preserve and restore Salem's physical and cultural heritage. In 1966, the United States Bank of Oregon rebuilt the Ladd and Bush Bank in much of the nineteenth century design. Others restored the Pacific Northwest's oldest remaining structures, Jason Lee's home and parsonage, and the John D. Boon house beside the old Thomas Kay Woolen Mill, itself being restored. In 1975 the finely landscaped Deepwood joined Bush House to exemplify the town's Victorian era. In addition, the old Reed Opera House became the centerpiece for shops in the Reed Opera House Mall.

Salem, during the 1960s and 1970s, acquired or improved other institutions which reflected its status as an appealing mid-sized city. Willamette University added stature, enrollment, and new facilities. From its staff, Salem native Mark Hatfield rose to state and national office. Western Baptist College and a large Chemeketa College opened their doors. The two hospitals enlarged, then merged administrations. A public broadcasting station began eleven years of television originating from Salem. A new National Guard Armory provided a badly needed auditorium. The State Fair, despite poor quarters, drew vast crowds with big-time entertainment and farm- and home-oriented events.

Volunteers made the arts flourish. The Salem Arts Association conducted year-round events, including a summer arts festival, and it opened the Art Barn. The Pentacle Theater gained a permanent home. Salem added a new Youth Symphony, a pops orchestra, and the Argonauts Drum and Bugle Corps. From the Salem Community Symphony, a paid Salem Symphony Orchestra developed. Bracketing the ages, Salem inaugurated a Boy's Club and a Salem Senior Center with an active Salem Area Senior organization. Proud to be the state capital, Salem and its people continue to build and to enrich their city—and to enjoy it.

The award winning "All-America" Salem of 1961 reached eastward into the broad Willamette Valley toward Mount Jefferson and across the river into Polk County. Courtesy of Oregon Department of Transportation

Hurricane-like winds on October 12, 1962, brought massive damage throughout the Salem area. The Columbus Day storm toppled trees onto cars at the fairgrounds and elsewhere. Courtesy of Statesman-Journal

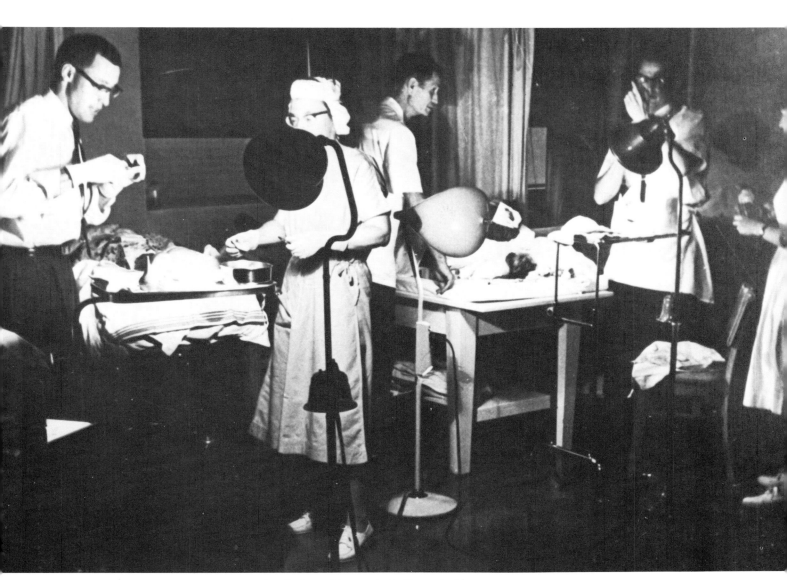

At Salem Memorial Hospital, a second emergency room facility handled the torrent of injured from the Columbus Day Storm of 1962. Courtesy of Statesman-Journal

Willson Park lost many trees and emerged terribly battered by the Columbus Day Storm. The state acquired ownership and on September 27, 1966, rededicated and improved Willson Park. The First United Methodist Church is at its border. Courtesy of Salem Public Library/ Maxwell

Allen Tompkins received oxygen while others continued battling the flames of a fire in the 1900 block of Northeast Commercial Street on August 2, 1977. Photograph by Robert DeGuido, courtesy of Statesman-Journal

The Willamette River flooded in December 1964 almost as badly as it had in 1861. Water ran from downtown to Interstate 5. As Pringle Creek rose over its banks on December 23, the National Guard evacuated nearly 300 people from Salem Memorial Hospital. Sergeant Larry Penrod carried the newborn child of Mr. and Mrs. Joe Garcia from it. More flooding hit Salem and the hospital in January 1965. Photograph by John Ericksen, courtesy of Statesman-Journal

Women packed beans, the main vegetable crop around Salem in 1960, at Blue Lake Packers at 325 Northwest Patterson Avenue, now Agripac. In the mid-1970s, mechanization of can lines ended much hand labor and greatly shrank numbers hired seasonally. Courtesy of Salem Area Chamber of Commerce

Gould National Battery was a World War II addition to Salem. In the 1960s, an employee handtested batteries. Gould Inc. is now at 576 Northwest Patterson Avenue. Courtesy of Salem Area Chamber of Commerce

All ages attended a Chemeketa College peace rally on May 10, 1972. Salem remained relatively quiet during the stormy 1960s and 1970s. Courtesy of Statesman-Journal

The grape boycott picketers, who had been arrested for supporting the United Farm Workers, were released from the Marion County jail on Thanksgiving Day, 1968. By the 1970s a small Hispanic population had settled in Salem, more in Woodburn. From Oregon Historical Society/ Oregon Journal

The Oregon Pulp and Paper Company in January 1960 brought oil by barge to make steam and to end the cinders harassing south Salem for years. It was the first freight shipped by river since 1938. Courtesy of Boise Cascade Paper Group, Salem, Oregon

From the 1920s until the December 1964 flood permanently closed the Boise Cascade chipping operation beside the river, Salem's paper mill turned logs into wood chips to make pulp for paper. Chips came by truck until 1982, when the box plant and paper converting facility alone operated. Courtesy of Boise Cascade Paper Group, Salem, Oregon

Company officials photographed Boise Cascade's final digester "blow" of choking odors into Salem on December 13, 1973. By 1980, the plant had invested about $10 million battling water and air pollution. Courtesy of Boise Cascade Paper Group, Salem, Oregon

There were at least two smiles for the camera during a too-predictable traffic jam on the Center Street bridge, July 15, 1970. Wanting a third Willamette bridge, Salem, instead, added approaches to both bridges on the Salem side. Courtesy of Statesman-Journal

A modern Salem moved its boundary to along the interstate highway as development, here at the Market Street interchange on September 18, 1972, spread to it and beyond. Courtesy of Statesman-Journal

Salemtowne, an adult community photographed in 1969, opened on the cleared Wallace farm in 1967. It became part of Salem mainly to obtain city water and sewer connections. Courtesy of Salem Area Chamber of Commerce

Robert S. Wallace began raising fruit west of Salem in 1886 and soon claimed the largest pear orchard on the Pacific Coast. When it was owned by his son, Paul Wallace, part of the farm about 1900 adjoined Wallace and Brush College roads. Courtesy of Oregon State Library

Meeting or not, the legislature is always "news" for Salem and the state. A photographer used a "fish eye" lens in the House of Representatives in 1978 to give an encompassing sense of the important institution. Photograph by Ron Cooper, courtesy of Statesman-Journal

Tom Gosnell, a tree cutter, posed during the 1970s in a light-hearted imitation of The Pioneer atop the Capitol. Courtesy of Statesman-Journal

The Capitol, symbol of Oregon, rises above older symbols on the Mall, December 25, 1961. Courtesy of Statesman-Journal

Pringle Park in 1979 set off the State Accident Insurance Fund Building at the edge of downtown. Photographed by Linda Berman, courtesy of City of Salem

The state continued to add new buildings and more personnel in Salem throughout the 1960s and 1970s. An office in the Labor and Industries Building already seemed jammed in 1961, the year of its opening. Courtesy of Statesman-Journal

Oregon State Employees Association picketers at the Capitol on May 8, 1975. As the Oregon Public Employees Union, the thirty-eight-year-old union today represents about 20,000 state employees. Teamsters and others represent still other employees. Courtesy of Statesman-Journal

John E. Horner watched Doris Powell aid young cerebral palsy victims learn to stand at the Fairview Training Center in 1960. By 1980, thirty-eight of the largest, and over twenty smaller, state agencies employed some 15,000 people in the Salem-Marion County area. Photograph by Alfred A. Monner, from Oregon Historical Society/Oregon Journal

A class met in 1965 at the Oregon Correctional Institute, an intermediate penal institution opened in 1959. It stresses rehabilitation of first-time minor felons. The Oregon Women's Correctional Center opened next to the penitentiary in 1965. Courtesy of Statesman-Journal

Relaxation at the Oregon State Penitentiary in 1975 included reading a book on a gangster. In March 1968 inmates had burned sections of the older prison during a major riot. Courtesy of Statesman-Journal

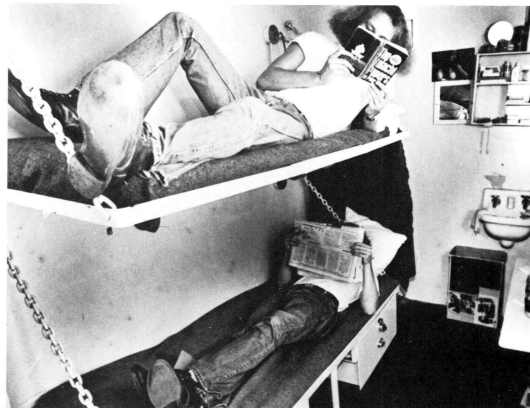

Beef Hereford judging underway at the 1971 State Fair repeated a scene familiar there for over 100 years. That year, the fair was largely a patched-together operation, its future in question. In 1980 its attendance set a record, propelling it from thirty-ninth to nineteenth largest among a thousand North American fairs. Courtesy of Oregon State Fair

Arleigh Birchler stood with his foot on Preston Morrow in Happy Birthday, Wanda June at the Pentacle Theater in April 1977. Since 1964 the community group has occupied a handsome structure in the Eola Hills designed by Charles Hawkes and built by volunteers. Courtesy of Statesman-Journal

High school students drawn from the west and Alaska played Tuneful Game at the federal Chemawa Indian School in 1972. In 1971 it reached a peak enrollment of 600 and has since built a new and enlarged campus. Chemawa is the nation's oldest residential school in continuous operation off reservations for native Americans. Courtesy of Statesman-Journal

Seven artists displayed their talent on the Courthouse grounds in 1950, and in 1953 the Salem Art Association acquired sponsorship on the Bush House grounds of the Salem Art Fair and Festival. Pictured in 1976, the July weekend event had grown in displays and popularity. Forty thousand have attended recent fairs. Photograph by Russ Trohmeyer/ Courtesy of Statesman-Journal

The Salem Saddle Club began in 1939 at the fairgrounds and later built its own stables and arena for horse shows and other activities at 2115 Southeast Cordon Road. Courtesy of Salem Area Chamber of Commerce

Salem built an impressive Civic Center on one-time Gaiety Hill in 1971-1972. City Hall rose above the Mirror Pond in August 1972. Courtesy of Statesman-Journal

The Civic Center, which also includes the Public Library and Fire Hall, appeared serene in an aerial photograph before landscaping was complete. Courtesy of City of Salem

Neighborhood groups and government combined during the 1960s and 1970s to reverse neighborhood deterioration. Oak Hill Apartments provided new low-income housing at Oak Hill and Southeast Twelfth streets on December 22, 1981. Courtesy of Statesman-Journal

Salem experienced its greatest period of park and recreation expansion during the 1970s. From an earlier day, the sequoia planted by William Waldo in 1872 at Northeast Summer and Union streets became tiny Waldo Park. Courtesy of Al Jones

Wallace Marine Park, pictured, was the city's sole waterfront park during the 1950s and 1960s. Heightened demand for river recreation led to its extensive development, after damage during the December 1964 flood, into the Albert-Wallace Willamette Memorial Park. Courtesy of Salem Area Chamber of Commerce

Children crossed a temporary Pringle Creek bridge in Bush's Pasture Park in 1969. Salem made the creek, elsewhere buried beneath streets and hidden behind neglected buildings, into a prominent, attractive urban feature during the 1970s. Courtesy of Statesman-Journal

The Pringle Creek Urban Renewal program was tied to Salem's rejuvenation of streams and parks. The renewed area in 1975 included a pedestrian-bicycle path network through park settings, with the Capitol as backdrop. Courtesy of Statesman-Journal

Modern play equipment was part of Richmond Park in 1974. Courtesy of Statesman-Journal

Minto-Brown Island Park and Wildlife Refuge opened in 1978 and is partially developed. Photograph by Linda Berman, courtesy of City of Salem

A jogger in winter 1979 used the Minto-Brown jogging trail, almost ten miles long. Photograph by Linda Berman; courtesy of City of Salem

At Northeast Church and Center streets in 1978, another building downtown goes up to join, among others, the seven-story Equitable Center (opened in 1975), the Chemeketa Parkade (in 1978) and, in two years, the Nordstrom Mall. New building continues today. Photograph by Ron Cooper, courtesy of Statesman-Journal

This beautiful Victorian mansion, Deepwood, built for Dr. Luke A. Port in 1894, became successive home for George and Willie Bingham, Clifford and Alice Brown, and then Keith Powell before opening to the public in the 1970s at 1116 Southeast Mission Street. Elizabeth Lord and Edith Schryver, Oregon's first women landscape gardeners, helped Alice Brown develop acres of fine gardens. Courtesy of Statesman-Journal

The Reed Opera House Mall exemplified a new use for old buildings. Centered around the original Reed Opera House, the complex of shops, including this Reed Wine and Cheese Shop in 1976, also linked with a smaller structure built to its south in 1902 and with the former Montgomery Ward Company store of 1936. Photograph by Gerry Lewin, courtesy of Statesman-Journal

Salem during the 1960s and 1970s saved some buildings with architectural and historic merit. By 1975 the Mission Mill Museum complex at 260 Southeast Twelfth Street included the Thomas Kay Woolen Mill and warehouse. It also moved to the property the now restored Jason Lee House and the Jason Lee Parsonage (both from 1841) and the John D. Boon House of 1846. Courtesy of Statesman-Journal

The spinning wheel and furnishings are in the Jason Lee Parsonage at the Mission Mill Museum. The Lee house and parsonage are two of the three oldest buildings in the Pacific Northwest. Courtesy of Statesman-Journal

A 1979 open house in the Learning Resources Building at Chemeketa Community College attracted many Salemites. Opened by the Salem public schools in 1954 as Salem Technical Vocational School, it became the separate Chemeketa Community College in 1970. Photograph by Kit Purdon, courtesy of Chemeketa Community College

Students practiced fire protection and trauma-reducing skills during a car wreck exercise in 1975 at Chemeketa Community College. Courtesy of Statesman-Journal

Between 1942 and 1967 President George Herbert Smith broadened Willamette University's traditional orientation to Salem and Oregon into programs with an outlook of national scope and reach. The library in 1975 remained its quiet core as university enrollment, staff, endowment, and quarters grew. Courtesy of Willamette University

Losers of the 1979 Freshman Glee waded the Mill Race, as tradition demanded. In 1996, Willamette University's Freshman Glee, the nation's oldest (1909) original song and dance college competition, ended. New records were in the making. In October 1997, the university fielded the first woman to play in an American college football game. Courtesy of Willamette University

Chapter Seven

The Capitol Mall blossomed in 1998 after a decade of changes. A grassy park covered a new underground garage. Beyond the Mall (right middle distance) the Human Resources Building had risen. So too, just above it, had the Edwards State Archives, and almost across, the State Land Building. The Public Utilities Commission occupied the remodeled Sears store, to the right. Courtesy of Oregon Department of Transportation

1980–1998

The Oregon Defense Forces Bagpipe Band regularly draws admirers at the Salem Art Fair and Festival. By the late 1990s, the several-day July event had grown to attract more than 100,000 visitors to juried arts and crafts shows and to the performing arts. Courtesy of Salem Convention and Visitors Association

Willamette University's Mark O. Hatfield Library (pictured), honoring the senator and former student and faculty member, opened in 1986, and the F. W. Olin Science Center, in 1996. In these decades, the university intellectually and materially boosted its undergraduate and professional schools. It also created the most culturally diverse student body and campus environment in its long history. Photograph by Dale Peterson; courtesy of Willamette University

Important changes mark Salem since 1980. The city has more and different people, more and different businesses, housing and institutions, more and different employment. Parts of Salem look different now than in 1980 because they are different. Historic continuity also marks Salem. Being a state capital constantly shapes its existence. Being a vibrant, friendly, clean, and attractive place is still important. Being near other growing towns and cities still offers advantages and disadvantages.

Nature still lavishes its bounty—and imposes its costs—on Salem. It benefits from a mild climate, regional agricultural riches, good water and power resources, and a wealth of outdoor recreation. It suffers through occasional natural disasters. In March 1993, the "spring break" earthquake damaged the Capitol and its surroundings; it did worse harm to nearby towns. Then, floods in February 1996 poured torrents of water, mud, and debris into Oregon rivers and streams. Some Salem streets and houses were inundated. The city's water treatment plant on the North Santiam River faltered under the muddy onslaught. Everybody was asked to cut water use in half for two weeks. Yet compared to earlier ravages, this flood was a gentle one for Salem.

Noticeable changes marked Salem's most recent twenty years. Salem's big population boom in the 1970s slowed in the early 1980s because of a national recession. In 1983, the number of Salemites declined for the first time in memory. Growth began again in 1987 and 1988. It was fueled by natural increase—more births than deaths—and even more by individuals and families moving to the area. To a large extent, people came because Salem and its region offered more and sometimes better jobs than competitors. Over 89,000 people lived in the city in 1980, and more than 124,000 (est.) in 1997. Marion and Polk counties, composing metropolitan Salem, achieved a higher growth. Area population rose from almost 250,000 in 1980 to over 324,000 (est.) in 1997.

Salem has become more ethnically and racially diverse in the process. Hispanics, African Americans, and Native Americans make up a larger percentage of Salem now than they did in 1980. A wave of Southeast Asians had arrived in the 1970s and continued in the early 1980s. New customs, institutions, and individuals gained promi-

nence in the community. Churches offered foreign-language services and programs; ethnic businesses multiplied; new cultural expressions appeared. Important Asian-owned or managed firms opened. In these years Chemeketa Community College became one of the most ethnically and racially diverse places in Salem.

Like the nation itself, Salem grayed. Individuals lived longer than before. As well, older people migrated to the city. Between 1985 and 1990 there was an influx of retirees drawn to Salem's mild climate, affordable housing, and pleasant living. Organized retirement communities and care homes spread. The city by the late 1990s had a higher percentage of those over age sixty-five than the rest of the state. Older people became a more forceful presence in Salem.

Salem earned its living after 1980, as before, mostly in trade, services, and government sectors. Residents continued to concentrate heavily in administrative and clerical occupations. Governments, schools, and hospitals remained the biggest employers. The State of Oregon topped the list with more than 18,000 people on its area payroll. Beginning about 1983, Salem, like the Pacific Northwest, moved away from making and handling wood products. Boise Cascade Corporation's local paper operations shrank, for instance.

Food processing, especially of canned and frozen items, remained the biggest single manufacturing sector as the work forces at Norpac, Agripac, and other companies roughly tripled during the peak harvest seasons. But many of their competitors had disappeared from Salem by the mid-1980s as the number of food processors fell everywhere. There were also signs of diversity in Salem's historic food processing industry, such as meat processing at Kyotaru Oregon, and soy sauce brewing, at Yamasa Shoyu Company.

Considerable light manufacturing has located in Salem since 1980, prominently in new industrial parks and along highways. These companies make buildings, silicon wafers, fabricated metal products, electronic and navigational equipment, and recreational items. As magnets for suppliers and related businesses, they multiplied jobs more than the retail or service businesses. Numbers of them have foreign owners or engage in world trade.

Oregon's Silicon Forest branched into Salem, especially drawn by its pure water and cheap electricity. In 1980, Salem contained eight high-tech firms employing about 200 workers. By 1997, Mitsubishi Silicon America, which opened locally as Siltec Corp. in 1982, by itself employed over 1,200 people after making huge investments in plants and equipment. Salem now learned how national and international ups and downs keenly affected innovative high-tech firms—and their communities.

The Salem-based Northwest Children's Ballet Folklórico, founded in 1992, performs traditional and modern Mexican dances. Cinco de Mayo celebration of Mexican Independence at the Fairgrounds in 1997 similarly indicated the importance of Hispanic people and culture in Salem. The fastest-growing segment of Oregon in the 1990s, Latinos composed a tenth of Marion County by 1996, giving it the state's largest Hispanic population. Courtesy of Northwest Children's Ballet Folklórico

Tokyo International University of America opened a computer-equipped campus across from Willamette University in 1989. Students from its Japanese home university enroll for ten months of English language and American studies. Cultural exchange is furthered through shared classes and dormitories with Willamette University. Salem's Sister-City relations with Kawagoe, Japan, further strengthened the area's cultural and economic ties to Japan. Courtesy of Tokyo International University of America

Many Chemeketa Community College settings afforded students chances to enjoy and learn from one another and the faculty. The college celebrated a quarter-century anniversary in 1995. By the late 1990s, almost 40,000 students of all ages enrolled annually. Chemeketa offered over forty associate degree and certification programs, and just as many programs for those planning to transfer to four-year schools. Courtesy of Chemeketa Community College

Ross Sutherland worked in the climate-controlled stacks of the Cecil Edwards State Archives in 1998. Oregon's official documents are collected and preserved in this tourist-attraction building, opened in 1991. Professionals help patrons in the handsome David C. Duniway Reference Room. Government agencies historically are a major employer of Salem's professionals, a group often lending its talents to the city. Photograph by and courtesy of Julie Yamaka

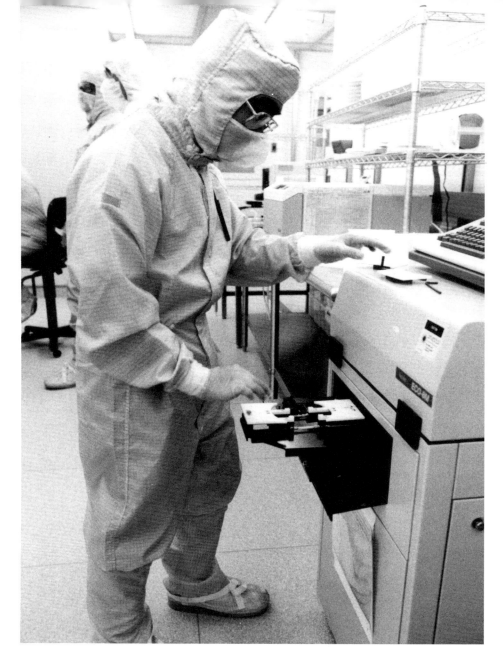

In 1986, an employee soldered a motherboard at II Murrow, maker of vehicle tracking systems. And at Siltec Corporation in 1990—now Silicon Mitsubishi America and Salem's largest manufacturing employer—a "clean room" worker prepared silicon wafers for the semiconductor industry. In the 1980s Oregon's high-tech Silicon Forest reached Salem, a historic light manufacturing center. Courtesy of Salem Economic Development Corporation

Another housing development goes up in West Salem in October 1997. Big population growth over two decades—an estimated 15.2 percent increase to 124,190 residents between 1990 and 1997 alone—multiplied Salem's subdivisions, houses, apartments, and roads. Neighborhoods changed. Fields, orchards, forests, and bucolic views disappeared, while land-use planners struggled to manage urban creep. Photograph by Jay Reiter; courtesy of Statesman-Journal

Housing development took off in Salem during the 1990s. Owning and renting rose in cost, slowing retirees' movement to the city. Added employers and people in the 1980s and 1990s translated into added buildings, denser traffic, higher school enrollments, more use of public services and facilities, more of about everything. Forests, fields, and orchards gave way to new structures and roads. Slow-growth sentiment surfaced. Growth-related issues began shaping city and county politics. City expansion through annexations became less possible in Oregon. Keizer, long considered a suburb, did not join Salem but incorporated in 1982 and sought its own identity. The Salem-Keizer School District came into being; the minor league Volcanoes debuted in a new Keizer stadium in 1997, drawing Salem fans.

In the meantime, Salem benefited from its heritage of public-private cooperation. Governments maintained heavy investment in transportation, parks, recreation, urban renewal, economic growth, and other sectors. Private and public interests together strengthened the historic downtown core and neighborhoods. In the 1990s, Liberty Plaza and Pringle Parkade opened with combined shopping, governmental, and parking facilities. The Salem Public Library main branch underwent major expansion and renovation. In 1982, the National Civic League again selected Salem as an All-America City. Similar to what won the 1961 city award, Salem was recognized for its extensive citizen participation in urban growth management, economic development and self-help projects.

Salem likes to picture itself as having a small-town feel, big-city attractions, and a great location. For nineteen years, Summer in the City events have promoted the specialness of the downtown. Substantial long-term private and public improvements have kept Salem's downtown a dynamic, popular place despite strong competition from other areas. Courtesy of Salem Downtown Association

"Kultura" performed at the April 1991 opening of Capital Community Television's studio, launching public access TV in the Salem area. More than 600 volunteers have now produced countless hours of programs over several channels. CCTV programs reflect the area's richly diverse interests, groups, institutions, and organizations. Photograph by and courtesy of Ron Cooper

Video and digital technology united in one of the innovative, hands-on programs and exhibits at the A. C. Gilbert's Discovery Village. Since December 1989, it has helped children think, learn, have fun, and be creative. Its Toy Hall of Fame displays the advertised Erector Set,™ American Flyer trains, and other inventions of renowned toymaker and Salemite Gilbert. An outdoor science center and a hands-on Discovery Garden promise new features. Courtesy of A. C. Gilbert's Discovery Village

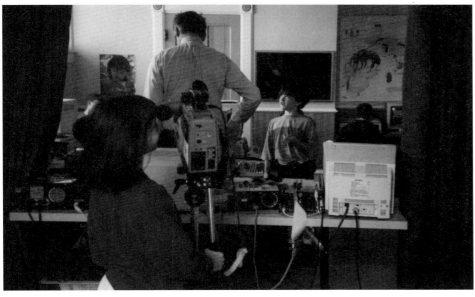

The city began transforming its neglected Willamette River backyard into a verdant Riverfront Park in 1996. This corridor includes an amphitheater, bike trails, paths, fountains, play areas, overlooks, and vintage buildings with new functions. A pavilion, fountains, and more pathways and overlooks are planned. Volunteers, in the old Salem tradition, helped create this waterfront recreational area. So too citizens contributed directly to neighborhood associations, to children's museum buildings, and to city, county, and state public services for older people, visitors, and others. (But they could not keep the Salem Symphony alive.) In 1987, a voluntary group of Oregonians purchased and renovated a big Tudor-style Salem home and presented Mahonia Hall to the state as Oregon's first official governor's mansion.

The State of Oregon, in a burst of activity initiated in the 1980s, integrated new, remodeled, and upgraded buildings into the 1990s landscape. Until then, almost 4,000 recently added employees had crammed into aging, inadequate state or rented quarters. Planners tried to create both useful and attractive buildings and outdoor spaces. A new State Lands Building opened in 1990, equipped with a grassy area, cobblestone courtyard and benches near Mill Creek. A showcase structure, the Edwards State Archives Building, opened nearby in 1991 for the preservation and use of the state's most valuable documents. The Capitol Mall acquired a new look. The Human Resources Building, opened in 1992, was second in size only to the Capitol. The Mall also gained a grassy park covering a new underground parking garage. And the Public Utilities Commission moved into the former Sears store nearby.

As the century neared its end, Salem was a thriving, confident and more complex place than ever before.

Mahonia Hall became Oregon's first official governor's mansion in 1987. Volunteers bought the stately half-timbered Tudor-style home, built in 1924 for hops grower and future Salem mayor Thomas Livesley. They renovated and refurbished the three-story mansion and donated it to the state. Volunteers now plan another refurbishment, one that honors its lavish oak trim and beams. Photograph by and courtesy of James B. Norman, Jr.

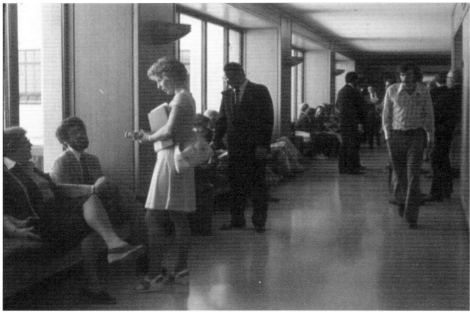

Every two years legislators, citizens, officials, staff, and the press cram the Capitol. Politics and governing never vacation, however. Neither does Nature. A 1993 earthquake knocked the Capitol tower's Golden Pioneer askew and damaged the Capitol Building. Handsome restoration, as of the rotunda dome, and rebuilding proceeded as legislators met in the basement. Courtesy of Legislative Administrative Committee/Information Systems; Rotunda courtesy of Salem Convention and Visitors Association

The 900-seat L. B. Day Ampitheatre opened in August 1987 for big-time professional entertainment at the Oregon State Fair. Some 680,000 visitors in recent years demonstrated its great drawing power each August. Crumbling facilities and financial difficulties still troubled the Fair's year-round operations. Courtesy of Salem Convention and Visitors Association

Riverfront Park is a new Salem feature in the late 1990s. It is transforming the neglected Willamette River backyard into attractive trails, paths, fountains, play areas, plantings, and outlooks. Artwork, an amphitheater, and vintage buildings given new functions also make it a lively showcase. Years in the making, the twenty-two-acre park will shape downtown development for years to come. Photograph by and courtesy of James B. Norman, Jr.

Afterword

I am grateful that numbers of people and institutions helped me expand my original pictorial history to treat Salem's history since 1980. At the *Statesman-Journal* Executive Editor Julia Wallace kindly opened its library files and gave me access to its committed newsroom staff. In it, Hank Arends and Larry Roby usefully discussed Salem's recent decades with me, and later reviewed my introduction to the final chapter. Retired journalist and longtime Salem historian Al Jones helpfully joined our discussions. Paula Fitch, its librarian, generously guided me through the newspaper's files and Salem's recent history and gave me other quite valuable assistance.

Edwin Peterson and Anna Peterson knowledgeably volunteered information about Salem's recent years and gave me their warm friendship. With humor and alacrity, City of Salem Public Information Officer Linda Berman provided photographs, suggested persons to see and places and events to consider, and gave me other very helpful aid. And Orrin P. Russie and James B. Norman, Jr., graciously went out of their way to furnish me their photographs.

For providing photographs or for other aid and encouragement, I thank Ted Burney, Ron Cooper, Barbara Dressler, Frank L. Evans, Bill I. Foster, Laurance E. Glassock, Christine M. Harris, Irene Hoadley, Abigal Lambert, Rosa Leonardi, Jennifer Madlad, Lin Murakami, Geof Parker, George Puentes, Karen Runkle, Ed Sobey, Ross Sutherland, William C. Sweeney, Eric Swenson, C. David White, Dave Wendell, and Julie Yamaka. I did not need to use the Marion County Historical Society for its recent *Statesman-Journal* photographs of Marion and Polk counties, but others should.

All the while, Diana Kerman has replenished me.

I have, in the meantime, sorely missed the presence of Salem's late, lamented David C. Duniway. He was a marvelous friend always ready to share his keen grasp of Oregon history and of living a good and worthy life: **In Memoriam**.

For Further Reference

A history of Salem, based on extensive, though scattered materials, is badly needed. Until then, here are some ways to learn something of Salem's past.

Work with the staff and in the catalogs at the Oregon State Library, Salem Public Library, and Oregon Historical Society. Be sure to see the Hugh Morrow Collection in the Salem Public Library, and for photographs, the Ben Maxwell Collection, including scrapbooks of clippings.

Selectively use *Marion County History* and *The Oregon Historical Quarterly*.

Read Robert M. Gatke, *Chronicles of Willamette* Vol. II (1970).

Enjoy Susan K. Seyl, comp., *The Art Perfected: Portraiture from the Tom Cronise Studio* (Portland: Oregon Historical Society, 1980) for selected portraits of Salem area people between 1880 and 1927.

Use the recent *Statesman-Journal* photographs for Marion and Polk counties at the Marion County Historical Society.

Index

A
Adams, Robert, 42
Agricultural Building, 26
Agripac, 165
Airplanes, 62, 77, 107, 115
Airport, 132
Alaska Gold Rush, 31, 51
Albert, John H., 25
Albert-Wallace Willamette Memorial Park, 183
All America City award, 156, 159
Allstate Insurance Company, 127
Alumina plant, 127, 139
American Legion, 115
American Legion Drum Corps, 107
American Red Cross, 146
Argonauts Drum and Bugle Corps, 107
Armstrong, Philo, 50
Art Barn, 157
Automobiles and trucks, 60, 61, 62, 64, 65, 89, 94, 97, 106, 109, 111, 120, 127

B
Babcock, Billy, 49
Babcock Furniture Store, F. J., 16
Baker, Colonel Edward Dickenson, 34
Barbord, "Mode," 38
Barnes' New York Racket Store, E. T., 72
Baumgartner, Joe, 54
Bennett House, 17
Bentley and Company, D. S., 68
Bigger, H. John, 50
Bingham, George H., 55, 186
Bingham, Willie, 186
Bingham, William, 55
Birchler, Arleigh, 178
Bishop, Charles P., 51, 73
Bishop's Store for Men, 73
Blacks, 13, 80, 156
Bligh's Capitol Theater, 116, 117
Bligh's Hotel, 74
Bligh's Theater, 65, 74
Blue Lake Packers, 165
Boarding Houses, 52
Boat building, 61
Boise, Reuben, 55
Boise Cascade Corporation, 19, 151, 169
Bonesteele, Russell, 156
Boon, John D., 16
Boon House, John D., 187
Boon's Island, 16
Boon's Treasury Tavern, 16
Booth, Rev. Robert A., 106
Boy's Club, 157
Boynter, George, 50
Bozarth, Scott, 45
Breyman Brothers, 25, 86
Breyman, Eugene, 30
Breyman, Jessie, 54
Breyman, Minnie, 30
Breyman, Werner, 55, 88
Bridges, 19, 33, 61, 64, 127, 148-150, 169
Broadcasting, 142, 157
Brown, Alice, 186
Brown, Clifford, 55, 186
Brown, Matt, 50
Brown warehouses, Clifford W., 113
Brown, William, 55
Browning Brothers Amusement Company, 121
Burnett, George, H., 55
Burns, Sandy, 21
Buses, 72, 106, 114, 127
Bush, A. N., 147
Bush, Ashael II, 147
Bush, Sally, 61, 147
Bush House, 128, 147, 157, 179
Bush Pasture's Park, 128, 184
Byrd, Dr. Prince, 64, 100
Byrd, Veda, 64

C
California, 12
Canneries, 76, 108, 113, 126, 140
Camp Adair, 126, 132, 135
Capital City Creamery, 87
Capital Community (CCTV), 198
Capital Journal, 107
Capitol Building, 12, 13, 24, 26, 30, 57, 86, 88, 89, 108, 122, 157, 174, 184, 202
Capitol Drug Store, 74
Capitol Mall, 174
Capitol Mills, 33
Capitol Tower, 11, 106
Case, Ethelbert C., 70
Castle and Cooke Foods, 140
Catholics, 25, 107
Chadwick, Stephen, 13
Chamber of Commerce, 115
Chamberlain, George, E., 89, 91
Chase, John, 36
Chemeketa Community College, 157, 166, 187, 188, 195
Chemeketa House, 11, 24
Chemeketa Indians, 12
Chemewa Indian School, 30, 179
Cherrians, 62, 117, 148
Cherringo, 117
Cherryland Festival, 128
Chinese, 13, 14, 30, 34, 60, 80, 107
Churches, 12, 13, 14, 25, 48, 60, 67, 92, 107
Churchill Sash and Door Manufacturing Company, 32
City government, 127
City Hall, 30, 123, 182
Civic Center, 182
Civil War, 14, 20, 34, 62, 131
Collins, George, 45
Columbus Day Storm, 156, 160, 162
Commonwealth Fund, 115
Community Concert Association, 108
Congregational Association, 48
Coomer, John, 36
Crawford, Ed, 36
Crawford, Henry R., 132
Cross, Curtis B., 68, 96, 100
Cross, E. C., 44
Cross and Son Market, E. C., 68
Crystal Gardens Ballroom, 106
Cultural life, 14, 30, 31, 36, 37, 62, 102, 103, 106, 107, 108, 143, 157
Curly's Dairy, 137

D
Day Ampitheatre, L. B., 203
Deaconess Hospital (Salem Memorial Hospital), 66
Delaney, Walt, 56
Dearborn, Dick, 45
Dearborn, Ella, 45
Deepwood, 157, 186
Depots, 32, 61, 63, 72, 76
Depressions, 31, 53, 107-109, 120, 122, 123, 126
Derrick, W. M., 102
Dole, 140
Drake, Benjamin F., 18
Dugan Brothers Plumbers, 50
Duniway Reference Room (State Archives), 195
Durbin, Sol, 20

E
East Salem, 13, 43, 61
East Salem School, 43, 149
Edwards State Archives, 195
Eisenhower, Dwight D., 147
Eld, Lieutenant Henry, Jr., 14
Elfstrom, Robert L., 143
Elks, 62, 88, 92
Elsinore Theater, 116, 117
Ely, Eugene, 62, 77
England, Eugene, 36
Englewood School, 115
Eyerly, Lee, 115
Eyre, David, 100

F
Fairview Training Center, 61, 84, 176
Farrar, Joe, 36
Farrar, John, 36
Fashion Stables, 45
Ferries, 26, 33, 64
Fire fighting, 17, 31, 43, 44, 65, 66, 106, 126, 128, 162, 182
Fire Hall, 182
Fires, 13, 14, 49, 51, 122
First Methodist Church. *See* Methodists
First National Bank, 106
First Presbyterian Church, 107
Floods, 12, 13, 31, 34, 47, 64, 87, 150, 163, 183
Fontaine Saloon, 46
Fraternal Order of Eagles, 121
Frederick and Nelson Department Store, 127
Freshman Glee (Willamette University), 189
Friends Polytechnic Institute, 30

G
Gabrielson, Carl, 100
Garcia, Joe, 163
Gardner, J. C., 23
Gardner Shackle, 23
Garrett, Armond, 132
George Waters Field, 130
Germans, 14, 30
Gideon Stolz Company, 113
Gilbert, A. N., 50, 54
Gilbert, Marietta, 48
Gilbert's Discovery Village, A. C., 199
Gill Bookstore, J. K., 11
Glaze, Rube, 36
Glen Oak Orphanage, 22
Gosnell, Tom, 174
Gould Inc., 166
Gould National Battery, 166
Graham fleet, 34
Grand Opera House, 103
Grand Opera Theater, 37, 61
Grants, 127
Grant School, 80
Griswold Block, 11
Grover, LaFayette, 13

H
Hamman Stage Lines, 72
Hars, Frank, 36
Hatch, George, 45
Hatfield, Mark, 157
Hatfield Library (Willamette University), Mark O., 192
Hawkes, Charles, 178
Health, 14, 38, 115
Hendricks, Robert J., 88
Highland district, 68
Highway Building, 128
Hillcrest School of Oregon, 61
Hirsch, Edward, 50
Hirsch, Gerty, 54
Hirsch, Leona, 54
Hispanics, 156, 157, 194

Hollywood district, 112
Holman, George, 25
Holman, Joseph, 25
Holman, Thomas, 56
Holman Building, 139
Holman ferry, 33
Holverson and Yantis' Men's Store, 25
Hoover, Herbert, 32
Horner, John E., 176
Hospitals, 24, 30, 157
Hoss, David, 142
Hotels, 14, 52
Howison, Lieutenant Neil, 12
Hrubetz, Frank, 141
Hunter, Roman, 68

I
Illahee Hills Country Club, 100
Illihee Country Club, 100
Indian Manual Labor School, 20
Irvine, J. D., 57

J
Japanese, 60, 80, 81, 126, 195
Japanese Community Church, 81
Japanese Hand Laundry and Dry Cleaning Works, 81
Jason Lee Home and Parsonage, 157, 187
Jews, 83
Judson, Lewis H., 14
Junior Symphony, 143

K
Kapphahn, Ernest L., 72
Kapphahn Transfer Company, 72
Kay Woolen Mill, Thomas, 127
Kelly, Harry, 16
Kibele, Louis, 56
K.O.C.O., 142
Korean War, 146
Ku Klux Klan, 107

L
Labor and Industries Building, 175
Labor Temple, 126
Labor unions, 60, 96, 122, 126, 127, 167, 176
Ladd and Bush Bank, 11, 25, 74, 123, 147, 157
Lai Yick, 80
Lee, Rev. Jason, 12, 14, 128
Legislature, 57, 139, 146, 173
Leslie, George, 65
Levy, Fred, 36
Liberty Theater, Ye, 88
Lindbergh, Colonel Charles A., 107
Lipman's Department Store, 127
Little, Professor, 54
Little Central School, 80
Livesley, Thomas, 201

Lone Oak Race Track, 84
Long, Ed, 36
Long, Fletch, 68
Long, Mack, 36
Long Range Planning Commission, 127
Lord, Elizabeth, 186
Lord, William, 30

M
McCrow and Willard Meat Market, 38
McCulloch Stadium (Willamette University), 144
McCully and Starkey Cash Store, 17
MacDowell Club chorus, 107
McElroy, William, 36
McIllwain, Curtis E., 21
McKay, Douglas, 147
McNary, Charles, 54, 129
McNary, John, 45
McNary Field, 115
Mack, George, 36
Mahonia Hall, 201
Marion County Courthouse, 17, 26, 86, 91, 126, 136, 148
Marion County Health Department, 115
Marion County Jail, 167
Marion Hotel, 26, 61, 65, 122
Marion Motor Hotel, 24
Marion Square, 12, 89, 108
Marion Square Bandstand, 143
Marshall, Willard, 156
Masonic Band, 36
Masonic Building, 61
Mauzey, Perry O., 38
Meier and Frank Department Store, 127, 147
Mellow Moon Dance Hall, 150
Merrill, David, 85
Meredith, Dr. W. J., 50
Methodists, 12, 14, 17, 20, 86, 106, 162
Meyer, Fred, 108
Meyers, George, 50
Meyers, M. L., 36
Miles Linen Company, 114
Mill Creek, 12, 118
Mill Race and Pond, 17, 99, 189
Mills, 12, 13, 17, 26, 32, 33, 61, 62, 66, 68, 106, 114, 126
Miller's Department Store, 106, 137
Minthorn, Dr. Henry J., 32
Minto, Frank, 123
Minto, Jasper, 45
Minto, John, 20
Minto-Brown Island Park and Wildlife Refuge, 185
Mission Mill Museum, 14, 51, 140, 187
Monarch Stove Factory, 84

Montgomery Ward Company, 186
Moore Business Forms, 127
Moores, J. H., 18
Morrow, Preston, 178
Motor Shop, 109
Movies, 62, 87, 88, 106, 116, 117
Moyer, Harry, 88
Murphy, Chester, 54

N
Nation, John, 18
National Guard, 44, 60, 61
National Guard Armory, 157
Native Americans, 20
Newspapers, 31, 40, 88, 107, 141
Newberry, 127
North, George, 140
North Mill Creek, 120, 152
North Salem, 13, 19, 61
North Salem School, 180
North Santiam River, 127
Northwest Children's Ballet Folklorico, 194

O
Oak Hill Apartments, 183
Odd Fellows Cemetery, 73
Odd Fellows Temple, 37, 45, 61, 103
Ohmart, Roy V., 73
Old Gaiety Dance Club, 101
Olcott, Ben, 54, 62
Oregon Correctional Institute, 177
Oregon Defense Forces Bagpipe Band, 192
Oregon Development League, 65
Oregon Electric Interurban Railroad, 61, 63, 72
Oregon Flax Textile Company, 114
Oregon Home for the Sick, 24
Oregon Institute, 13, 17, 20
Oregon Linen Mills, 114
Oregon Motor Stages, 114
Oregon Public Employees Union, 176
Oregon Pulp and Paper Company, 106, 118, 126, 151, 168
Oregon School for the Blind, 74, 121
Oregon Stages, 114
Oregon State Agricultural Society, 20
Oregon State Employees Association, 176
Oregon State Fair, 20, 31, 46, 51, 57, 61, 62, 74, 77, 93, 94, 102, 116, 145, 157, 160, 178, 181, 192, 203
Oregon State Hospital (Insane Asylum), 30, 50, 61, 84
Oregon State Library, 24, 122
Oregon State Penitentiary, 13,
23, 30, 84, 85, 177
Oregon State School for the Deaf, 142
Oregon Statesman, 14, 40, 88, 107, 141, 147
Oregon Telephone and Telegraph Company, 39
Oregon Women's Correctional Center, 177
Oregon Workers Alliance, 122
Oregon and California Railroad, 32
Oregonian, 141
Outdoor recreation, 14, 31, 45, 46, 54, 55, 60, 96, 97, 99, 119, 120, 157, 183-185

P
Pacific Christian Advocate, 21
Pacific Highway, 116
"Painless Parker" dentist, 74
Painter, Clare, 142
Palmer, Zadie, 45
Parades, 14, 31, 44, 60, 62, 77, 89, 121, 128, 131, 146
Parrish, J. L., 14
Parrish Junior High School, 106
Parry, Will H., 30
Patton, Harry, 132
Patton Block, 11
Paulus Brothers, 140
Penrod, Larry, 163
Pentacle Theater, 157, 178
Pickett, Margaret, 142
Pioneer Trust, 17, 74
Piper, Ted, 36
Pohle, Herman, 42
Police, 38
Politics, 14, 50, 60, 88-91, 129
Port, Dr. Luke A., 186
Portland Auto Club, 65
Post Office, 30, 45, 86, 107, 148
Potter, Theodore, 36
Powell, Doris, 176
Powell, Keith, 186
Pringle Creek, 18, 47, 163, 184
Pringle Creek Urban Renewal Program, 185
Pringle Park, 106, 175
Prohibition, 107
Public Library, 101, 182
Public Service Building, 128
Putnam, George, 107

R
Racing, 145
Railroads, 14, 19, 30, 32, 61, 63, 64, 66, 72, 76, 114, 116, 148, 149, 156
Raymond, William, 14
Reed Opera House, 14, 24, 37, 47, 61, 157, 186

Reed Opera House Mall, 24, 157, 186
Reed Wine and Cheese Shop, 186
Richmond Park, 184
Rigdon, Winfield T., 71
Rigdon Funeral Home, 70
Rigdon-Ransom Colonial Funeral Chapel, 71
Riley, Dick, 36
Riverfront Park, 204
River Traffic (*also see* Steamboats), 12
Roads, 14, 30, 31, 60, 61, 112, 126, 156, 170
Roosevelt administration, Franklin D., 121
Roosevelt, Theodore, 88, 89

S
Sacred Heart Academy, 30, 37
Safeway, 43, 111, 112, 113, 149
St. Joseph Church, 25
St. Vincent De Paul Church, 107
Salem Airport, 115
Salem Amusement Company Band, 36
Salem Area Senior organization, 157
Salem Centennial, 126, 128, 129
Salem Armory, 103
Salem Art Association, 128, 157, 179
Salem Art Fair, 179, 192
Salem City Band, 143
"Salem Clique," 14
Salem Community Symphony, 157
Salem Dodgers, 130
Salem Federal Arts Center, 108
Salem Federated Musicians, 143
Salem Flouring Mill Company, 17, 46, 68
Salem Hardware Company, 97
Salem High School, 14
Salem Hospital (Salem General Hospital), 22, 67
Salem Indian Training School, 62, 78
Salem Iron Works, 18
Salem Labor Exchange, 57
Salem Linen Mills, 114
Salem Memorial Hospital, 161
Salem Navigation Company, 120
Salem Philharmonic, 103
Salem Saddle Club, 181
Salem Senators, 106, 130
Salem Senior Center, 157
Salem State Bank, 74
Salem Symphony Orchestra, 103, 143, 157
Salem Technical Vocational School, 187
Salem Trades and Labor Council, 96
Salem Water Company, 51
Salem Women's Club, 100
Salem Woolen Mill Store, 73
Salem-Falls City and Western Railroad, 64
Salem as capital, 12, 13
Salemtowne, 170
Saloons, 21, 31, 46, 47
Savage, Burt, 49
Savage, Mark, 49
Schafer Blacksmith Shop, A. C., 42
School for Deaf Mutes, 56
Schovell, Dr. H. H., 62, 77
Schriber and Pohle Blacksmith Shop, 42
Schryver, Edith, 186
Scott, Captain Lyman S., 45
Sears and Roebuck, 108
Sharff, Don, 140
Sidewalks, 13, 25, 31, 60, 61, 112
Silicon Mitsubishi America, 196
Siltec Corporation, 196
Sites, Professor John, 103
Skaggs Grocery, 111
Smith, George Herbert, 188
Smith, Jim, 32
Smith, William Stephens, 56
Smith and Steiner Drugstore, 39, 50
South Mill Creek, 19
South Salem, 13, 61
South Salem High School, 128
South Salem Slough, 46
Southern Pacific Railroad, 32, 63, 114
Spa Restaurant, 52
Spanish-American War, 31, 51, 60, 86, 131
Sparks Center (Willamette University), 144
Spaulding Logging Company, 66
Spears, Frank, Jr., 100
Sprague, Charles A., 107, 141
State Accident Insurance Fund Building, 175
State Farm Mutual Insurance Company, 127
State Insurance Company, 31
Stallion show, 40
Staver, Rev. and Mrs. Daniel, 48
Steamboats, 18, 19, 26, 30, 33, 34, 36, 61, 62, 66, 120
Steinbock Junk Company, 83
Steiner, Albert, 50
Steiner, Armint, 50
Steiner, Lee, 50
Steusloff Brothers Meat Market, 87
Strong, Anna, 54
"Summer in the City," 197
Sun Lung (Laundry), 34
Supreme Court Building, 61
Sutherland, Ross, 195
Sweetland Field (Willamette University), 144

T
Taft, William Howard, 91
Talkington and Aiken Saloon, 47
Taylor, Ben, 45, 62, 77
Teamsters Union, 176
Temple Beth Sholom, 83
Thomas Kay Woolen Mill, 51, 127, 140, 157, 187
Tioga Block, 11
Tokyo International University of America, 195
Tompkins, Allen, 162
Tracy, Harry, 85
Trolleys, 31, 32, 50, 61, 74, 87, 106, 114
Tuberculosis Hospital, 61
Turner, Glen, 45
Twilight University, 108
II Murrow, 195

U
U.S. Bank of Oregon, 157
U.S.O., 133
United Air Lines, 132
United States Bank of Salem, 74
Utilities, 14, 25, 31, 39, 50, 51, 52, 56, 68, 107, 127, 157, 170

V
Valley Packing Company, 116
Vaudette Theater, 87
Volchok, Zollie, 117

W
Wade Farm Machinery Company, R. M., 21
Wade, William Lincoln, 16
Wait Hardware and Farm Machinery Store, T. B., 38
Waite Fountain, 61
Waldo, William, 183
Waldo Park, 183
Wallace, Paul, 171
Wallace, Robert S., 171
Wallace Marine Park, 128, 183
Waller (University) Hall (Willamette University), 20, 49
Washington School, 149
Waters, Franklin L., 88
West, Fred, 53
West, John Gulliver, 53
West, Nean, 53
West, Oswald, 53, 61, 88
West, Walter, 53
West Salem, 61, 64, 126, 127, 150, 152, 197
Western Baptist College, 157
Western Fanning Mill, 32
Western Paper Company, 106

Wheelock, Grace, 91
Wilkes Expedition, 14
Willamette Flouring Mill, 19
Willamette Hotel, 24, 30, 61, 65
Willamette River, 12, 14, 106, 120, 150, 151, 157, 163, 168
Willamette University, 12, 13, 20, 30, 48, 49, 85, 86, 103, 126, 128, 135, 143, 144, 157, 188, 189, 192, 195
Willamette University-Salem Community Symphony, 143
Willamette Valley Flouring Mills (Scotch Mills), 33
Willamette Valley May Festivals, 103
Willamette Woolen Manufacturing Company, 17, 19
Willoughby, A. O., 132
Wilson, J. J., 50
Wilson, Otto, 65
Wilson Park, 25, 26, 30, 60, 61, 86, 143, 162
Withycombe, Dr. James, 91
Woodmen of the World, 92
Woolworths, 74
World War One, 62, 64, 103, 108
World War Two, 126, 131-138, 166
Wright, George, 50

Y
Yew Park, 66
Youth Symphony, 157
YMCA, 30, 49, 107, 108, 135
YWCA, 101